The Goodwood
Phantom
Drophead Coupé

The Goodwood
Phantom
Drophead Coupé

Malcolm Tucker

The Goodwood Phantom
Drophead Coupé

by Malcolm Tucker

Published 2007

ISBN: 978-1-85443-229-2

Printed and bound in
Singapore by Star Standard

for the publisher

Dalton Watson Fine Books
1730 Christopher Drive,
Deerfield, IL 60015,
USA

www.daltonwatson.com

Acknowledgements

The writer of a book such as this sits at the centre of a circle. Around him are a multitude of people who make the work possible. In this case the circle consists of the Rolls-Royce Motor Cars directors, managers and staff who gave so freely and patiently their time, as they took part in interviews, explanations and site visits concerning their particular work on Project RR2, the creation of the new Rolls-Royce Phantom Drophead Coupé. It is these visitors to the circle, named below, to whom I express my sincere thanks and gratitude.

Ian Robertson, chairman and chief executive; Dr. Karlheinz Bierwirth, head of Project RR2; Ian Cameron, chief designer; Marek Djordjevic, chief stylist exterior design; Charles Coldham, chief interior designer, Alan Sheppard, interior design project leader; Sami Coultas, colour and trim designer; Kris Sukhu, surface integration manager; Hermann Bohrer, former director of manufacturing; Helmut Riedl, director of engineering; Olaf Kraschienski, spaceframe design; Clive Woolmer, head of powertrain engineering and bespoke division; Theo Martin, former head of testing; Siegfried Wesinger, durability testing, South Africa; Graham Biggs, director of corporate communications; Graeme Grieve, sales and marketing director; Paul Ferraiolo, marketing director; David Archibald, regional director; Stefan Conrady, former product manager; Giles Clayton-Jones, brand manager; Andrew Ball, corporate communications manager; Jonathan Stanley, product public relations manager.

A special thanks to the four people who guided me both physically and mentally through the corridors of Rolls-Royce Motor Cars in England and in Munich. At Goodwood, Matt Thornton, marketing communications manager and Samantha Cullum, marketing communications executive, at Rolls-Royce in Munich, Kathrin Aigner, project assistant and Soner Oguz, former intern.

A final word of thanks to my publishers, Glyn and Jean Morris of Dalton Watson Fine Books Inc, and to my editor David Burgess-Wise, whose skill at smoothing the rough-hewn word is here for all to see. To book designer Ben Gibbs, whose talent and imagination have greatly benefitted this book. Also, to Richard Newton whose inspired photography enhances the words throughout and to Paul Wood for providing historic photographs.

This book is dedicated to all the people who had the foresight to create the new Rolls-Royce Motor Cars Ltd and its current products, for without them the greatest name in automotive engineering may well have joined the ranks of lost causes in the British motor industry.

Contents

Introduction

At one minute past midnight on 1 January 2003, a hush fell over the New Year party at the just-completed head office and manufacturing plant of Rolls-Royce Motor Cars Ltd. All the guests, the workforce and their families gathered around the end of the production line to witness the owner of the first production Rolls-Royce Phantom take possession of his car. The company chairman handed over the keys, and as the applause died down and the party got under way again, the car slipped silently from the manufacturing plant into the chill night air and on to the empty roads leading from the Goodwood Estate, just north of Chichester in the quintessentially English county of West Sussex.

Less than five years earlier, by agreement with Rolls-Royce plc, at a meeting also attended by Volkswagen AG, the BMW Group had acquired the rights to use the name 'Rolls-Royce' and its linked 'R-R' motif, radiator grille design and Spirit of Ecstasy mascot. As the Silver Seraph generation of cars was still in production at Volkswagen AG subsidiary Bentley Motors, the deal stipulated that no BMW Group-produced car bearing any of the above features should be advertised or sold before 1 January 2003, which became the target date for the BMW Group to have established an autonomous Rolls-Royce division. Within that self-imposed five-year timescale, it had to find a suitable site on which to plan, build and equip a head office and manufacturing plant and design, test and build an entirely new car worthy of the Rolls-Royce name.

The first director of 'Project Rolls-Royce', as it was known in the early days, was long-time BMW employee Karl-Heinz Kalbfell. He had successfully lobbied for the car to be designed in its homeland, far away from the BMW culture in Munich. A design studio was set up in a former bank building on the north side of London's Hyde Park, where the heritage and historic values of Rolls-Royce could more easily be absorbed. Chief designer Ian Cameron was delighted with the arrangement, knowing that while all the resources of the BMW Group were available, they would not be thrust upon him. He had free rein to design the first completely new Rolls-Royce in six decades.

At first, the new car was simply known by the code-name 'RR01', but the senior members of Project Rolls-Royce eventually decided on a name with historic Rolls-Royce provenance – 'Phantom'. It was a wise decision, for the first new Rolls-Royce model under BMW Group ownership would be a large formal saloon, and Phantom suited it very well.

For almost thirty years, prior to BMW Group ownership, Rolls-Royce cars had long been designed and built under a tightly-controlled budget that thwarted the efforts of its designers and craftsmen to produce a vehicle that could truly be described as 'the best car in the world'. It was decided that RR01 would have to impress without compromise if that time-honoured Rolls-Royce motto was to ring true once more.

A large formal car, designed to appeal to royalty, high society, business people, entertainers and athletes, was seen as the best way to re-establish the marque in its premier position among potential customers and car enthusiasts the world over. The proof would be in how the car looked and behaved, and time has confirmed all – and more – than Rolls-Royce Motor Cars Ltd had wished, for the acceptance of the Phantom.

Time has shown the siting of the head office and manufacturing plant at Goodwood to be prudent, and the Phantom itself has proved to be a success, unreservedly as a motor car and cautiously as a source of revenue for the BMW Group. It was always known that the Phantom alone could not generate enough revenue to meet the cost of the Goodwood investment. Other models would be needed, and the Phantom's spaceframe construction has enabled that to happen in a cost-effective way, with a 250mm extended wheelbase version now also built at Goodwood. Additionally, the German coachbuilder, mutec, offers an even longer car with an extra row of rear-facing seats.

Even before RR01 was signed off for production, Ian Cameron had begun designing a two-door, four-seater convertible version. He proposed that Rolls-Royce build an experimental car to test public and press reaction. The company responded admirably, and on Tuesday 2 March 2004, '100EX' was unveiled at the Geneva Motor Show, receiving unprecedented acclaim and a very firm 'two thumbs up'. Following the hugely positive public reaction to '100EX', the BMW Group gave Rolls-Royce the go-ahead for a production version that would eventually be named the Phantom Drophead Coupé.

Towards the end of 2003, I was commissioned by Dalton Watson Fine Books to write a book about the Rolls-Royce saloon, entitled *The Goodwood Phantom*. This book, *The Goodwood Phantom Drophead Coupé*, is a companion to that first volume, as the Drophead Coupé shares much of the engineering design of the Phantom saloon. I have endeavoured to include only information from the first book necessary to give a satisfying account of the Drophead Coupé's design and engineering, but in some instances reference to the *Goodwood Phantom* volume will add to the reader's knowledge of detail, and it also includes information about the manufacturing plant itself.

Rolls-Royce set out to build the most striking, innovative and stylish drophead four-seater car ever. It is my hope that within these pages you will discover whether or not they succeeded.

Malcolm Tucker - Hampshire, UK, 2007

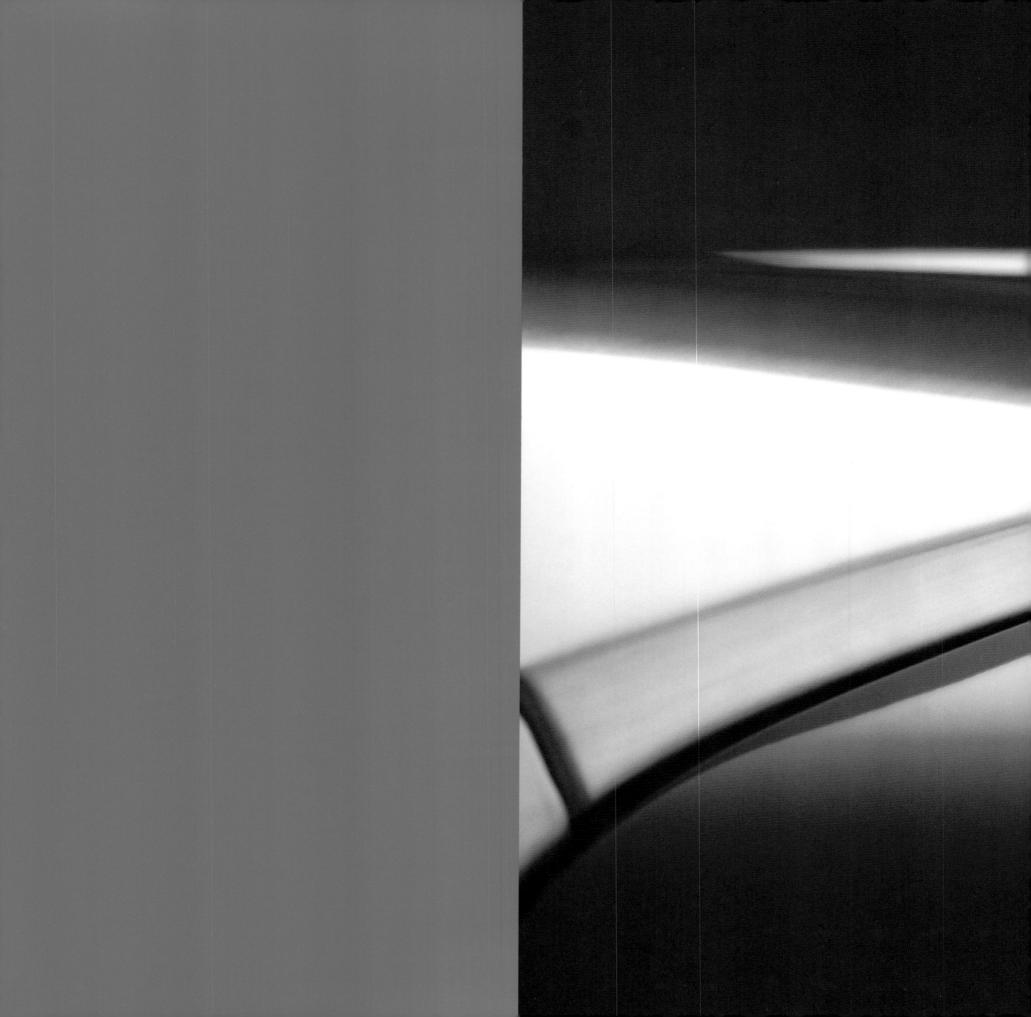

Chapter One
Driving The Drophead

First impressions of the Drophead Coupé are remarkable. One cannot help but be impressed. Chief designer Ian Cameron's masterful styling draws the observer up short, and it's all too easy to just stand and admire the car rather than slide comfortably into its driver's seat. The car is full of promise, just sitting on the tarmac; it radiates discreet power, finesse and excitement. Its taut lines evoke a noble lineage, the rising waistline over the rear quarters recalling that gifted designer John Blatchley's classic Rolls-Royce Corniche.

However, other features such as the boot handle, rear light clusters and large wheels are shared with the Phantom saloon.

Unexpectedly, there are few other external clues to indicate that this car is derived from the Phantom saloon. The swaged side panel and the arrangement of the front lamps, with rectangular auxiliary lights over round headlights, may be similar to the saloon, but they have now taken on a new identity.

Opposite: perfectly proportioned, the Drophead Coupé excites attention from any angle. Its wide rear-hinged doors allow excellent access to the cosseting back seat.

Above: a new look for a familiar shape. While the radiator shell retains the traditional 'Parthenon' form laid down by Sir Henry Royce in 1904, it now leans slightly backwards to impart a sense of movement, even when the car is at rest.

Right: while the taut lines of the Drophead Coupé evoke a noble lineage, with echoes of the classic Rolls-Royce Corniche, they have a distinctive character of their own.

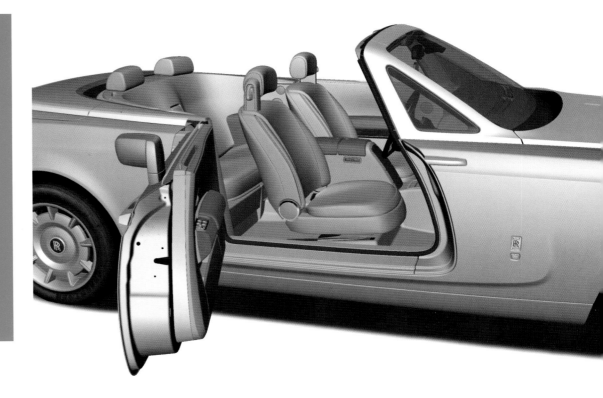

Opposite: as it is designed as a high-speed tourer, Rolls-Royce decided to endow the Drophead Coupé with the largest wheels fitted on any production passenger car in the interests of ride comfort and style.

Right: in this early rendering, classically-proportioned lightweight sporting seats support their occupants on smooth leather surfaces that recall the upholstery of fashionable cars of the 1930s.

"Such amazing life and responsiveness tend to make almost any driver safer than ever"
Wilfred Gordon Aston on the Phantom II, 1929

The familiar radiator shell nestles gently into the wing panels and bonnet top, and while it retains the traditional 'Parthenon' form laid down by Sir Henry Royce over a century ago, it now leans slightly backwards – a first for a Rolls-Royce production model, lending the car a sense of movement, even when at rest. The brushed stainless steel bonnet leads the eye back to the satin-polished stainless steel windscreen surround and quarter-light frames. Polished stainless steel and teak door cappings flow into the embellishing strip that encloses the rear teak decking, while the entire shape reflects the nautical inspiration of the Drophead Coupé's styling.

Inside and out, the look follows a more curvaceous theme than the Phantom saloon. Seats, armrests and door trim are just some of the elements that incorporate this curvilinear emphasis, shared by many of the external styling features. It's a relaxed design without aggressive undertones. The Drophead Coupé offers a welcoming and sociable environment.

Ian Cameron set out to create a car that would make travelling an engaging experience for the passengers as well as the driver. It is a combination of the car's ride quality and interior design that achieves this. Even comparatively minor details like the exterior door handles, more substantial and sharply defined than those of the sister Phantom, have a distinctive beauty. Strength, confidence and security are words that come to mind when using them.

Opposite: the 'lounge' rear seat is an intimate environment for two flanked by vertical storage cabinets. The hood mechanism is neatly concealed below a hand-crafted teak cover.

Above: raised, the cloth hood of the Drophead Coupé enhances the car's sporting lines while giving adequate headroom for front and rear passengers. The balanced lines bear witness to near-perfect weight distribution.

The wide rear-hinged doors allow excellent access to and from the back seat, especially as buttons and levers atop the front seats allow them to be moved forward and tilted out of a rear passenger's way.

Even with the top raised, access is good. All but those with the very longest torsos will have sufficient headroom in the back, and such is the range of the front seat adjustments that the headroom and driving position can be arranged to suit virtually any driver or passenger.

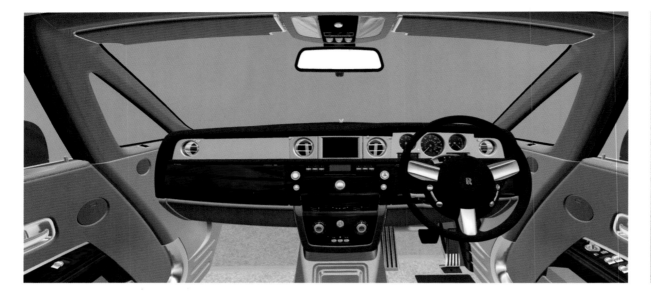

"The impeccable road behaviour and perfect suspension contribute to give the impression of a construction, the finish of which has no equal"
Charles Faroux of l'Auto on the Phantom II Continental, 1930

Once driver and passengers are seated, the doors can either be shut as normal by pulling on sculptured recesses in the door tops, or closed automatically by a button set ahead of each door. This system is sensitive to obstructions, thereby avoiding injury or damage to property. Either way, the 'soft closing' mechanism smoothly completes the action without the solid 'clunk' that those with long memories liken to the closure of a 'slam shut' railway carriage door.

Within seconds, driver and passengers will become conscious that the seats are about as comfortable as a car seat can be. Although the back rests are not as deep as those of the Phantom, they are carefully contoured to support the human form. Even very tall people will find these seats more relaxing than those of the Phantom, which are themselves extraordinarily good.

Once the seat and steering wheel positions have been set for optimum comfort and control, one elbow falls naturally on to the door armrest, ahead of which are the window lift and mirror controls. The other elbow can be supported by the centre console, which houses the controls for seat adjustment and seat warming as well as the 'violin key' lever that controls the opening and closing of the soft-top. This lever and the windscreen-frame mounted interior-lighting console are the only two significant differences between the controls on the Drophead Coupé and the Phantom.

Above left: the perfect driving environment, with all the controls and dials exactly where the driver would expect them to be.

Above right: neat 'violin keys' such as this raise and lower the windows and the hood.

Opposite: hand-crafted wood and leather interior trim is available in three combinations; 'Standard', 'Mono' and 'Linear', the latter inspired by Rolls-Royce's one-time stablemate, Riva boats.

Above: supplementing the mirrors is an advanced proximity-warning system that gives both audible and diagrammatic signals. It also provides a 'live' view of the car's extremities through rear-facing, and front sideways-facing cameras.

Left: with the hood up, rearward visibility through the rear window may be less than on the saloon, but careful design and high-mounted door mirrors mean that there are no dangerous blind spots.

The soft-top interior is of the finest quality material, and appears as rigid as a saloon's head-lining, only the sculptured shape and lack of window frames revealing that one is sitting beneath a cloth soft-top. There are no draughts and no tendency for the soft-top to billow outwards as speed increases, just a barely perceptible wind noise from the top corners of the windscreen frame. Though the necessarily smaller rear window of the drophead soft-top and the seat head-rests tend to restrict the view in the internal rear-view mirror, there are no dangerous blind spots when it is used in conjunction with the high-mounted door mirrors.

Visibility when reversing with the top up may be relatively limited, but the Drophead Coupé has both audible and diagrammatic proximity-warning systems incorporated in its Controller-activated monitor, and the same screen can also give a 'live' view of what is happening at the car's extremities thanks to rearward facing and front sideways-facing cameras.

On near-freezing days, the owner of a convertible car might be tempted to leave the soft-top up, but this would be a mistake in the Drophead Coupé. At the simple lift of the operating switch, the soft-top opens, folds and stows itself beneath the rear deck. There are no clips to loosen, nor is there a need to open the windows a fraction – the car does it all by itself. Many open cars minimise the space occupied by the stowed top by raking the windscreen frame back sharply. This may shorten the front extension of the folded soft-top, but it encroaches on the driver's space, especially for a tall person, bringing the top screen rail mere inches from his or her head. Not so in the Drophead Coupé, which succeeds in combining a relatively upright screen angle that allows plenty of headroom with a top that folds into a shallow compartment without intruding into the luggage space.

A touch of the switch causes the top to start its elegant disappearing act. No clips need to be loosened; the hood simply opens, folds itself up and stows itself away beneath the teak rear deck as if by magic. It only takes a few seconds.

"I must go down to the sea again…" And the nautically inspired styling of the Drophead Coupé is surely the perfect reason to take the words of the poem littorally…

The Drophead Coupé's occupants are not isolated from the world outside, but somehow their senses are only aware of those images, sounds and scents that are pleasing. No open car is at its best in a fume-filled city, but the sheer height of the Drophead Coupé, with roof down, windows up and air conditioning on, will be cushion enough to enjoy a chosen townscape. Out of town on a winding road, be it country or coastal, with dappled sunshine and the smell of new-mown grass or salt sea air, the fortunate occupants of a Drophead Coupé will be close to heaven on earth.

Once seated, the driver can absorb his or her first experience of the 'Authority Concept' developed to give the driver and passengers the ultimate feeling of well-being. The concept lay at the core of the design brief when Rolls-Royce Motor Cars developed the new Phantom. It starts with the driving position itself. Once adjusted, the seat allows a commanding view of the road ahead, with the subtly rounded bonnet in full view and the Spirit of Ecstasy radiator mascot leading the way. The windscreen and quarter-light frames may be substantial, but they do not needlessly intrude on forward vision. The clearly defined wing tops allow the car to be placed with precision.

Start the engine, and as the warning lights cycle on and off, the forward-opening doors are secured by an electronic interlock system that cannot be overridden by the handles once the car is travelling above 3mph. Having selected 'Drive' and checked the rear-view mirrors, a light but firm pressure on the throttle pedal urges the car silently forwards. At 30mph, the breeze is gently making itself felt, although on a freezing cold day, the car's heating system effortlessly counteracts nature. Increase the speed to the British legal limit of 70mph and the driver may feel the need to raise the side windows. Then the airflow into the cabin is kept at bay sufficiently for the exposure to the elements to be enjoyed.

The steering wheel and pedals are absolutely central to the driver's seat. The hands naturally grasp the large, thin-rimmed wheel with its satin aluminium spokes at the 'ten-to-two' or 'twenty-to-four' position, giving relaxed and comfortable control. The horns are sounded by depressing either of the upper two spokes, with the hi-fi, mobile telephone and satellite navigation system activated by chromium buttons on the hub.

One only has to reach out for the naturally anticipated position of a control, and there it is. Rolls-Royce calls this feature of its 'Authority Concept' the 'Intuitive Control', which is designed to give balance, proportion, precision, alignment, ease of control and harmony, when using the car's controls.

Left: a relaxed and comfortable journey is assured by the commanding driving position of the Drophead Coupé, with the steering wheel and pedals positioned directly in front of the fortunate driver.

Opposite: the elegant, uncluttered layout of the dashboard of the Drophead Coupé places the driver firmly in control.

Rolls-Royce has recognised that available technology can easily lead designers to provide a confusing overabundance of secondary controls. At the same time, higher road speeds and denser traffic make the manipulation of these additional knobs, buttons, levers and touch-sensitive screens increasingly dangerous.

In this car, primary controls are intuitive. Want to select a radio station? Push the large, gleaming chrome knob directly below the radio and turn for volume. Choose from the six pre-set stations by depressing one of the switches styled like violin tuning keys set three either side of the frequency display. All the other audio controls are in the same area but are shaped differently so that the driver's eyes do not need to leave the road ahead – the sense of touch is enough. Similarly, the air conditioning controls are grouped neatly below the main fascia.

Temperature is controlled by wheel-type dials rotating about a vertical axis and fan speed by knobs rotating about a longitudinal axis; it's all so simple. When the organ stop controls of the traditional 'eyeball' air vents are moved, they actuate tiny motors that slowly open the vents, avoiding an unseemly rush of air into the car's interior.

Secondary controls are conspicuous by their apparent absence. They come under the heading of 'Functionality upon request.' Some, like the electric seat adjusters, are concealed in compartments in the centre armrest; many are operated by the Multi-Task Controller (MTC). Similar in concept to BMW's proven 'I Drive' system, the MTC is a metal knob concealed in the front of the central armrest. Open its compartment and the dash-mounted clock panel rotates to reveal a monitor screen. The display can be altered by turning the MTC forward, back and to left or right, as well as pushing it downwards. The menu options displayed on the screen mimic the movements of the MTC, reinforcing once again the intuitive concept of the Drophead's design.

Rolls-Royce has retained its traditional switchbox for ignition key, starter button and lights, although the classic panel conceals the latest technology. Likewise the gear selector, mounted on the right of the steering column with a central 'annunciator' display visible through the steering wheel, is a familiar feature of every previous model since the Silver Shadow.

Concealed within the central armrest but available upon demand are secondary controls such as those regulating the seating positions.

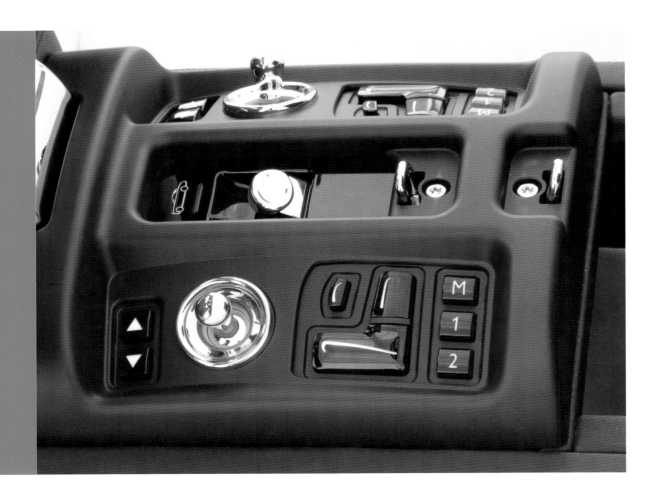

Opposite: six 'violin key' controls enable the driver to select a pre-set radio station at the touch of a finger. Here form follows function, so that the driver's eyes do not have to leave the road when the choice of entertainment is made.

Right: when the front panel of the central armrest is opened to reveal the Multi-Task Controller, the analogue clock on the dashboard rotates out of sight to reveal the MTC screen. The movements of the knob on the armrest are mimicked on the screen, giving the driver command over vehicle configuration, entertainment, navigation and communication.

Left: all is well with the world. A drive through the beautiful countryside of California's Marin County, and back across the Golden Gate bridge into San Francisco for dinner. Providing the car can beat the city's famous fog rolling down the hillside.

Above right: when driving an open car, the occupants are much more in touch with the surroundings, one effect of which is the changes in air temperature that will be experienced whilst driving along. On this narrow bridge spanning a canyon, you can be sure that a relatively cool breeze will be a welcome break from the heat of the twisting hillside roads.

Below right: another use for fine wood; this time planned by an architect rather than a car designer. Just as the Phantom Drophead Coupé is an example of traditional materials used in an modern way, so is the house.

Left: perfectly at home in any environment, the new Drophead Coupé epitomises Sir Henry Royce's vision of a car with "a bit of fizz."

Opposite above: throughout the long life of the Rolls-Royce marque, 'waftability' has been a defining virtue of every car's method of progress.

Opposite below: the carpet chosen for the Drophead Coupé may look like wool, but it is a man-made floor covering. Here, it is protected by a sisal matt.

The slightest tremor is detectible as the engine starts, but once the correct operating temperature has been reached, only the instruments reveal that the engine is running. The speedometer is set directly ahead of the driver, flanked on the right by a combined fuel and temperature gauge and on the left by a novel instrument – a type of rev-counter in reverse – that discreetly displays the percentage of engine power available.

The electronic gear-selector is used to choose Park, Drive, Neutral or Reverse, returning to its central position when released. The annunciator panel has three visible indicators; R, N, D, the fourth – P – appearing when chosen; in each case the selected letter is self-illuminating. The direction indicators are operated conventionally with a stalk on the left of the steering column, although if you wish to cancel the signal, then another push in the same direction is required.

As with gear selection, these tasks soon become second nature. When pulled back, the stalk also flashes the headlights. Screen-washer and wiper functions are operated by a similar arm below the gear-selector lever, and cruise control is engaged by a stalk beneath the direction indicator.

The throttle pedal has perfect balance and tension for smooth and rapid acceleration. The transmission is configured to move as quickly as possible through the six gear ratios, seamlessly making the most of the low down torque, or power produced at low engine speeds. This is one of those exceptional cars where the surrounding scenery appears to move past at an almost indecent rate relative to the efforts made by the driver and the machine. The commanding position, the excellent forward view encompassing the crests of both front wings and the apparently unlimited power combine for a driving experience that is second to none.

Although the only major changes made to the Phantom's mechanical components for the Drophead Coupé are the suspension settings, and the 9.5 inches /225mm reduction in wheelbase length, the latter contributes much to its sprightlier handling.

The car's performance can be fully appreciated on British 'A' class roads when conditions allow overtaking. To enable full use to be made of the low-speed engine torque, the gearbox selects top gear as soon as it can and holds it as long as possible while the throttle is fully depressed. Indeed, a driver unaccustomed to the car's potential may wonder if the kickdown is working. In reality, the world outside the car will be slipping past faster and faster, and the transmission will eventually drop a gear or two if 'emergency' acceleration is called for. Likewise, when the throttle is eased, the available torque will defer a downwards gear change.

Even under spirited acceleration, the exhaust emits no more than a discreet and pleasant burble.

All the while, the 'available power' dial shows the percentage of power quietly waiting to be unleashed. Cruise along at the 70mph British national speed limit and the 'available power' dial will show over 90 per cent. Who knows how high a speed or how steep a gradient would see its needle move down towards zero? It is the feeling of consummate ease with which the car performs that allows its occupants to enjoy the environment and the isolation from the world outside.

Narrow twisting lanes pose no problems for this Drophead Coupé. The steering feel and gearing allow the driver, giving due consideration to others, to flick the car around obstacles almost like a sports car. This feeling of security is aided by the computer-controlled air suspension that permits only a modicum of body roll, the amount of which is designed to minimise the effect of G force upon the car's occupants. The powerful brakes can reduce speed in an astonishing manner and of course the steering and suspension continue to imbue a feeling of control in almost any situation.

Potholes and other surface imperfections are rendered negligible by the adaptive suspension system combined with the rigidity of the spaceframe. You can see the bump coming but the car absorbs just about everything. Driver and passengers may hear a muffled thump, but they will feel little; feedback to the steering wheel and the sense of control that the driver experiences are just about perfect. How Rolls-Royce has managed to isolate the more unpleasant aspects of poor road surfaces and yet retain such a dynamic feel to the steering is remarkable. The engineers have succeeded in finding the ideal balance of control, performance and pampered comfort.

Over the years Rolls-Royce designers have demonstrated a clever knack of making their cars feel a great deal smaller to the fortunate person at the helm, than they actually are. The Drophead Coupé has continued this worthy trait, which is quite an accomplishment in today's dense traffic. All of the above aspects make driving the Rolls-Royce Phantom Drophead Coupé a unique experience, and for all the right reasons.

Even when driven in a leisurely manner the Drophead Coupé feels like the thoroughbred it is. Whereas the Phantom does all you ask of it in style, the Drophead Coupé adds the elements of nimbleness and willingness to do more and more when required. Decide to press on and drive in a more spirited fashion and it will reward the driver with a feeling of complete satisfaction in controlling a mighty machine. The car's ability to follow its front wheels in a turn defies the weight of such a large car, never giving a moment's concern to an experienced driver. The sheer willingness of the Drophead Coupé to master the road almost seems to imbue it with the sentient quality of a pure-bred racehorse – and a good-natured one at that.

Never intended to be a sports car with the attendant compromises in ride comfort, this grand tourer will enable a driver to cover great distances at high average speeds and arrive at journey's end not only feeling fresh and relaxed, but stimulated by the experience.

The Drophead Coupé is, then, a different driving experience from its progenitor Phantom. It is not that the variation of sensation between the two cars derives from myriad uniquely tuned components, because that is not the case; neither car is better than the other. They just fulfil diverse roles, and in each case the sum of the parts is different rather than greater. To drive the Drophead Coupé is without a doubt the epitome of self-indulgence, and to be driven in the Drophead Coupé is a close second, for Rolls-Royce has succeeded admirably in making a journey in this car a pleasure in a class of its own.

Above: the teak used in the rear decking, whose black caulking recalls the polished decks of classic America's Cup yachts, is hauled out of the jungle by elephant, for if it was floated down river impurities in the water would cause discolouration of the wood.

Right: with its grille merging into the bonnet and wings to a greater extent than on any previous production Rolls-Royce, the Drophead Coupé marks a major step forward in the aesthetic of the marque.

Chapter Two

A Century
Of Open-Top
Rolls-Royce Motor Cars

Ask any member of the public to draw an image of a Rolls-Royce car and they will probably sketch something akin to the Silver Cloud model built between 1955 and 1965, such is the iconic status of that more than fifty year-old design. Sporting, open bodywork does not come readily to mind when the name Rolls-Royce is mentioned, but in reality nothing could be farther from the truth. In the early days of the company, at the beginning of the last century, nearly all makes of car were fitted with open coachwork, although by the middle of the first decade, large closed limousine-style bodies were available on the more powerful chassis. Many of the open bodies were large and heavy, although they could often be most attractive. A few were light, stylish and rakish, their reduced weight being the main reason for a given chassis' enhanced performance.

From its introduction in 1906, the only mechanical difference between an open 40/50hp Rolls-Royce and a limousine built on the same chassis would have been the rake of the steering column and the rating of the road-springs to accommodate the different weight. The company's managing director Claude Johnson successfully demonstrated the performance of the 40/50hp by entering three open cars – the 'Silver Ghost', 'Silver Rogue' and 'White Knave' – in the Scottish Reliability Trials. The 'Silver Ghost' then went on to complete a 15,000-miles reliability trial of its own, in which it only made one unplanned stop, when a fuel cock vibrated shut. Johnson's gimmick of naming the cars certainly did no harm in endearing them to the motoring public of the day.

The classic vision of the Rolls-Royce – the Silver Cloud of 1955, perhaps the finest design created by John Blatchley during his long career as Rolls-Royce chief designer.

Above right: the most famous car in the world: the original 40/50hp 'Silver Ghost' built in 1906, tackling a Scottish by-road on the 90th anniversary of its triumphant 15,000 mile trial of 1907.

Below right: the Hon C.S. Rolls drives the Princess of Monaco in a 1905 20hp Rolls-Royce.

Below: first to wear the classic Rolls-Royce radiator was the little 10hp model introduced in 1904.

"I should like to have a Rolls-Royce car with enough petrol and tyres to last me all my life"
Lawrence of Arabia

In July 1911, Royce developed an experimental 'speed' car, chassis number 1701, for Johnson to use in a publicity campaign. Perversely named 'Sluggard', it ran non-stop in top gear from London to Edinburgh, under the supervision of the Royal Automobile Club. It differed from previous 40/50hp chassis in having a higher compression ratio and a larger carburettor, along with a revised rear-suspension layout. The increased engine power and superior handling, enhanced by a super-light open body, allowed the 'Sluggard' to reach 78mph and average fuel consumption of 24mpg between the two capital cities. Fitted with an even lighter streamlined body, it attained a speed of 101mph on the famous Brooklands motor racing circuit, south of London.

Production versions of 1701, known as the London-Edinburgh model were offered as an alternative to the standard cars, and further development resulted in the Continental chassis. These were capable of cruising at 70mph and were commonly known as the Alpine Eagle after a Continental won the 1913 Austrian Alpine Trial. So successful was the Continental that it became the basis for the standard model after World War One.

The London-Edinburgh and Alpine Eagle models established a precedent of open, sporting Rolls-Royce cars for most of the next 100 years.

The first post-World War One experimental Silver Ghost, as all the 40/50hp cars had become known, was built in 1919, being given the designation '1EX'. This suffix was used for large horsepower experimental chassis up until 1958, the last being '45EX', a Phantom V. By 1925, the Silver Ghost was showing its age and a new model replaced it. The 40/50hp New Phantom had a very similar chassis to the Silver Ghost but was powered by an entirely new overhead-valve engine of 7,668cc. Royce was aware that extra engine power was often cancelled out by fitting heavier bodywork, so he arranged for New Phantom '10EX' to have a light body with low wind resistance built to a Rolls-Royce design by Barker & Co. Its rear aspect may not have been particularly elegant, but it was certainly more aerodynamically efficient. Chassis '15EX', '16EX' and '17EX' were all fitted with similar bodies to prove Royce's point that increased performance and handling were achievable if customers were willing to sacrifice luxury.

Opposite above left: Sir Henry Royce's first "car with a bit of fizz" was the 40/50hp London-Edinburgh model, built to celebrate a famous top gear run between the two capitals in 1911.

Opposite above right: Claude Johnson, the commercial genius behind the Rolls-Royce motor car, who marketed Sir Henry Royce's superlative creations with flair and imagination.

Opposite below: the New Phantom experimental car, '16EX' was built to prove Sir Henry Royce's theories on increased performance and improved handling.

The New Phantom became known as the Phantom I when the Phantom II was introduced in 1929. During its production run of six years, many exquisite examples of the coachbuilders' art were fitted to the chassis, for this was the time when design stylists and engineering achievement seemed to be at their most compatible. Perhaps the most interesting version of the Phantom II was again named Continental. The car had a six inch shorter wheelbase than standard, and weight distribution over the axles was an important consideration to enable the design purpose of fast trans-Continental touring to be achieved. An experimental version of this car, '26EX', impressed Rolls-Royce Motor Cars chief stylist exterior design, Marek Djordjevic so much that he incorporated some of its design elements into the Goodwood-built Phantom.

Until 1935, Rolls-Royce motor car design was firmly rooted in Royce's mantra, 'Take the best that exists and make it better. When it doesn't exist, design it.' Cutting-edge technological innovations were rarely adopted, since proof of their long-term reliability and superiority was demanded. The Phantom III of that year could not be criticised for lack of innovation, as it featured a brand new V12 engine, a cross-braced cruciform chassis and independent front suspension. The new 7,340cc engine was more compact than its predecessor, but could propel a car fitted with not-too-heavy coachwork at 100mph. Yet it produced so much torque at very low speed that it was quite comfortable in top gear at just 4mph. The shorter power unit was installed farther forward than earlier designs, which allowed a more

spacious passenger compartment without an increase in wheelbase. This, of course, changed the visual balance between bonnet and passenger compartment, which the coachbuilders found easier to address on more sporting, convertible bodywork.

Since 1922, Rolls-Royce had offered a smaller model designed for the owner-driver alongside the Large Horsepower chassis, for it was felt that after the First World War there would be less demand for cars that needed a chauffeur to drive and maintain them. Royce was ever hopeful that bodies on the Small Horsepower chassis would be light and compact, allowing the less powerful engine to give more than adequate performance. However, so popular were the little 20hp cars that the coachbuilders soon started fitting large limousine and saloon bodies as these relatively less expensive cars encroached on the market for the Silver Ghost and Phantom I. More power was needed, and in 1929 the 20hp gave way to the 20/25hp, with the 25/30hp succeeding this in 1936.

The final pre-Second World War version was named Wraith, and had the benefit of the features found on the Phantom III chassis, though the engine was the same as that of the 25/30hp. The need to cater for more cumbersome coachwork endowed cars fitted with lighter bodies – tourers, doctor's coupés and dropheads – with livelier performance and a lightness of handling that the larger horsepower cars did not possess.

Above left: in 1922 Rolls-Royce introduced a new, smaller model, the six-cylinder 20hp seen here with fashionable Doctor's Coupé bodywork whose windscreen foreshadows that of the new Drophead Coupé.

Above right: a Phantom II of the early 1930s with stylish 'three-position' drophead coachwork.

Opposite: the wonderful flowing lines of Rolls-Royce coupés of the 1930s were a rich source of inspiration for the designers of the new Drophead Coupé, whose design acknowledges the past while looking resolutely to the future.

A year after the Second World War ended, Rolls-Royce introduced the Silver Wraith. It was an entirely new car, very different from the pre-war Phantom III. The V12 was dropped in favour of a 4,257cc six-cylinder engine, but the rolling chassis still had to make its way to a coachbuilder to be clothed in a body of the owner's choice. The car was really more suited to the role of luxurious saloon or limousine, although some drophead bodies were ordered and for the most part looked good. In 1949 a sister car appeared, with a wheelbase some seven inches shorter. Named the Silver Dawn, it was the first Rolls-Royce to have a factory-fitted body. This was a four-door saloon. Even so, some chassis' were still supplied to outside coachbuilders upon demand. The Silver Dawn looked particularly fine with open two-door four-seater bodywork.

In 1955 the Silver Cloud took over. Its 'standard steel' body is regarded as one of the most stylish cars ever to have gone into production. Still built with a separate chassis, it also provided the basis for the last efforts of many coachbuilders. Few dropheads were built, but those produced by H. J. Mulliner and James Young are truly beautiful examples of the coachbuilders art, whatever the period.

Elegant as it was, the Silver Cloud lacked modernity, even at its launch, and by 1965 it was truly outdated. The replacement featured Rolls-Royce's first chassisless semi-monocoque construction, where the entire body shell gave the car its strength and rigidity, and therefore had to be made as a complete vehicle. This type of construction was the final nail in the coffin of the traditional coachbuilder, for little could be done to alter the shape of the integral body shell. The Silver Shadow was launched as a four-door saloon, but in the same year two-door fixed-head and drophead coupé versions were created by Mulliner, Park Ward, by then merged into one company as a subsidiary of Rolls-Royce.

The formal elegance of a 1953 Silver Wraith, first new Rolls-Royce model introduced after the Second World War in 1946.

Above: the Silver Cloud III launched in 1962 marked the end of an era, for its 1965 replacement, the Silver Shadow, was the first Rolls-Royce to have a semi-monocoque.

Right: since 1950, her Majesty Queen Elizabeth II has used Rolls-Royce motor cars. In March 1966 the Queen and Prince Philip rode in this handsome Silver Cloud II Drophead with coachwork by H. J. Mulliner when they visited Nassau in the Bahamas.

On 4 February 1971, Rolls-Royce went into receivership due to inadequate accounting methods in the development of the RB211 turbofan aero-engine. The aero-engine company was quickly nationalised to safeguard the supply of military engines to the British government, but the future of the car division was in serious doubt. The managers at the car production facility at Crewe, Cheshire wondered whether to cancel the announcement of the Corniche, an updated two-door Silver Shadow. However, they went ahead with the press launch, using the French coastal road from which the car took its name as the location for the event. The Corniche was an immediate success, and the car division, having demonstrated its determination to survive, was successfully floated as a private company on the London Stock Exchange.

Controversial in design when new, the Silver Shadow is now regarded as being one of the most attractive 'three-

box' saloons (bonnet, passenger compartment, and boot) ever produced. The raised 'coke-bottle' waistline over the rear quarters of the Corniche enhanced that well balanced look, making both fixed-head and drophead versions far more graceful and desirable than their four-door counterparts.

Defence manufacturer Vickers plc bought Rolls-Royce Motors Ltd in 1980 as the Silver Shadow and its derivatives were being superseded by the four-door Silver Spirit range, which was actually a new body shape on the Silver Shadow floor pan. Thus the Corniche models could remain in production. Indeed they had to, as the retooling costs for a low volume two-door car would have been too expensive.

By 1991, a relationship was forming between Vickers and BMW, who advised on body rigidity, paint technology and air conditioning systems. Three years later, development

Opposite: immediately successful, the 1971 Corniche brought new grace to the Rolls-Royce range.

Above: in 1999, Rolls-Royce introduced a new Corniche, an exclusive drophead version of the Silver Seraph model.

work on the replacement for the Silver Spirit range was well under way, and BMW agreed to assist with designing the production line, as well as various components within the car. In the end, the German company became responsible for over thirty per cent of the components in the 1998 Silver Seraph, including its V12 engine. The Silver Seraph was a most attractive design. Featuring styling cues from the Silver Cloud and Silver Shadow, it was the first totally new Rolls-Royce since the 1946 Silver Wraith, but it did have two serious flaws: restricted interior space and an engine that did not deliver its power in the way expected by Rolls-Royce owners.

The year after the Seraph's introduction, the drophead coupé version appeared, featuring the upswept waistline that had become the hallmark of the Corniche.

The Seraph interpretation – which retained the Corniche name – was perhaps even more attractive. However, only 374 Corniches were built during the Seraph's four year production run.

The introduction of a new two-door, four-seater drophead coupé is therefore very much in the Rolls-Royce tradition. The fact that it is derived from an existing model is also very much in keeping with precedent. In the past, such a body style adapted from a saloon had always been compromised in terms of rigidity, leading to inferior handling characteristics as well as rattles and shakes, factors which were not acceptable to the new Goodwood-based Rolls-Royce Motor Cars. In theory, the torsional strength attained by adapting the Phantom's aluminium spaceframe would overcome these problems.

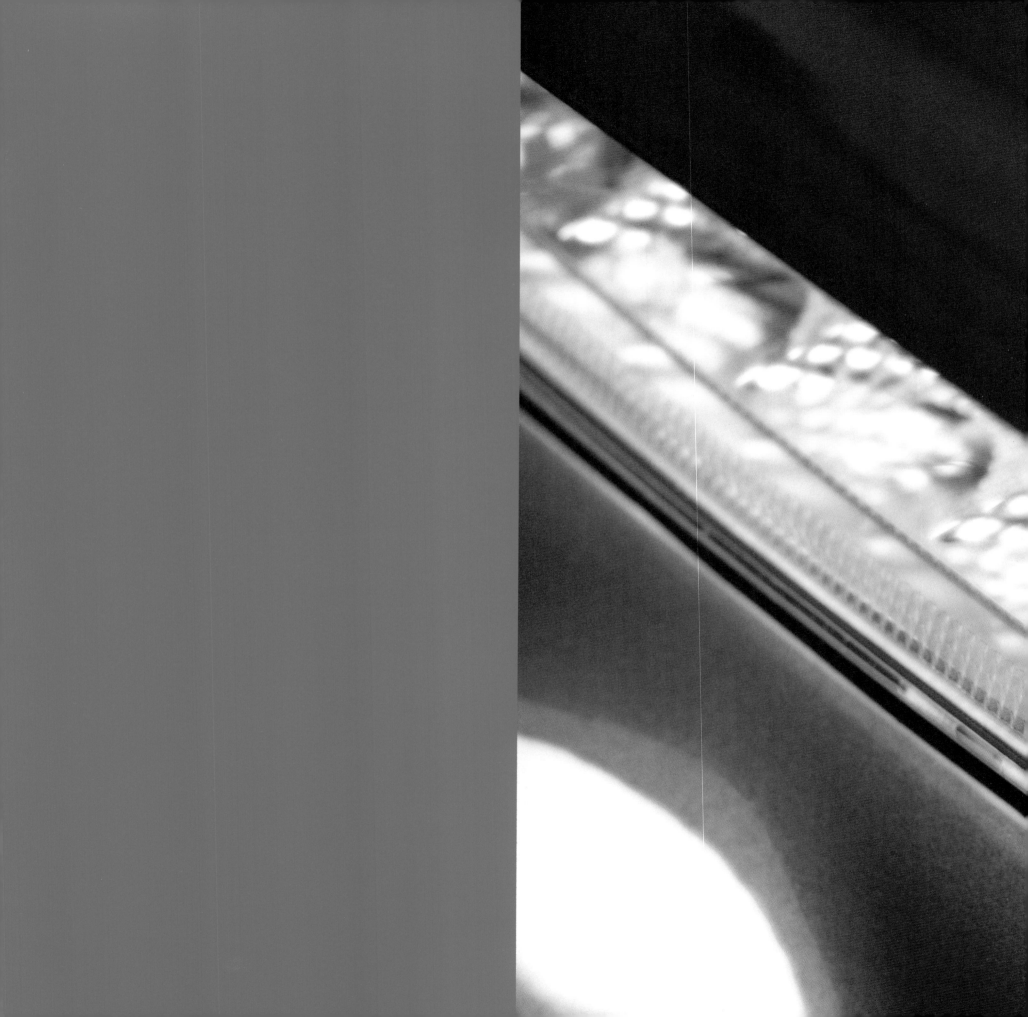

Chapter Three
The Philosophy Behind A
Soft-Top Rolls-Royce

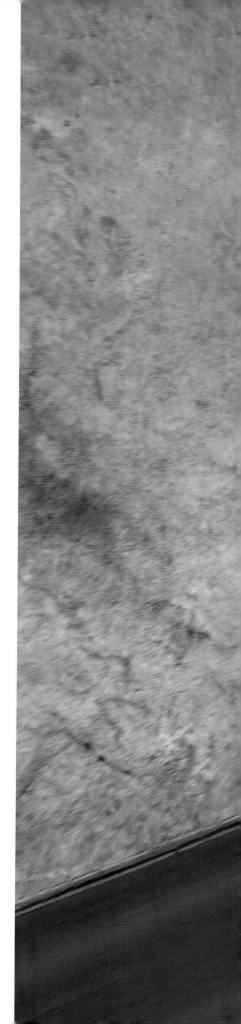

"In the words 'Rolls-Royce', you have a unique possession"
Lord Northcliffe, 1921

The genesis of the Drophead Coupé was in the late summer of 2001, long before the Phantom design was finalised, and only a few months after planning consent for the Goodwood manufacturing plant was granted. As there was no formal Rolls-Royce board of directors at that time, all major decisions were taken by the BMW Group board. To help them make informed judgments, the Project Rolls-Royce advisory team – known as the 'UR Circle' – was given the task of examining possible variants of the Phantom that utilised its aluminium spaceframe construction.

One of the choices put before the board was a two-door, four-seater drophead coupé. The board gave the go-ahead for a preliminary study group to review the feasibility of such a design. Led by a product strategy representative, Dieter Budde, the working group consisted of representatives from engineering, marketing, finance and purchasing. They addressed such matters as the engineering challenges, marketing requirements and the potential sales volumes in adapting the Phantom spaceframe. How different could such a car be from the parent Phantom? Of course, the finance team would cast a shadow over the whole procedure, for however fine the end product might be, if it could not add to the profitability of the future Rolls-Royce Motor Cars, it would never be built. Stefan Conrady, the marketing representative

on the working group, explained how they decided: "All the members would meet to define tasks, discuss matters within the group and take homework away. They would each liaise with relevant people within the fledgling Project Rolls-Royce team and the BMW Group. They would then come back with answers, which allowed the feasibility study to take form. It was initially hoped that the study would be completed in about three months of weekly meetings, and a recommendation would be put before the BMW board. In the event, the entire process proved to be more complicated than anyone had expected. This initial phase ultimately lasted for two and a half years. It was the summer of 2004 when we got the green-light to go ahead with the Drophead Coupé."

In January 2002, early on in the process, chief designer Ian Cameron, chief engineer Karl Baumer and Stefan Conrady visited Southern California to experience the environment in which many owners of convertible cars live. They met up with Marek Djordjevic of Design Works USA, who would take on the role of exterior designer for the new car, originally code-named RR02, but for convenience was soon renamed RR2. They drove the then-current Rolls-Royce Corniche, a Lexus SC430, and a Bentley Azure. The Bentley was hired from a rental company, whose representative suspected they wanted to use the car in a film of dubious content.

Just the sort of road that the Drophead Coupé was designed for. A winding twisting two-lane highway climbs up a California hillside before dropping down into the wine country of the Napa and Sonoma valleys. Of course a trip along the Corniche of Southern France, or an Alpine road in summer would be as welcome.

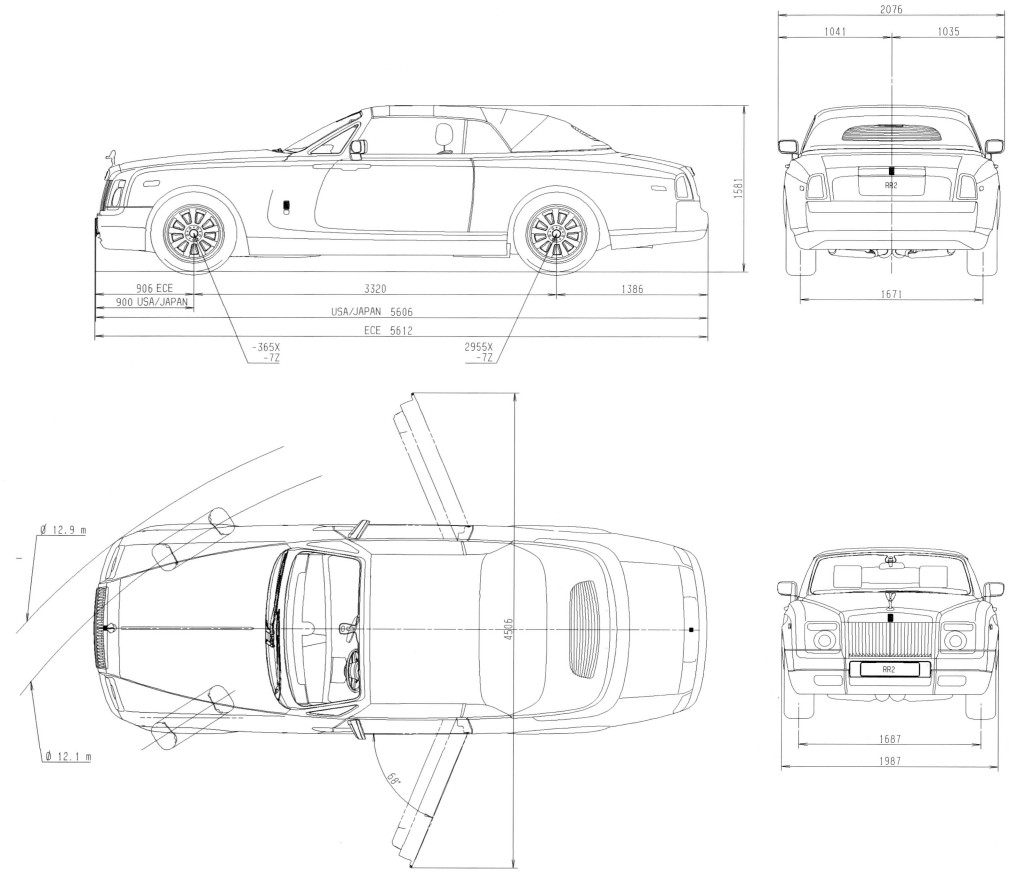

906 ECE
900 USA/JAPAN

3320

1386

USA/JAPAN 5606

ECE 5612

-365X
-7Z

2955X
-7Z

1581

2076

1041

1035

1671

Ø 12.9 m

Ø 12.1 m

4506

68°

1687

1987

58

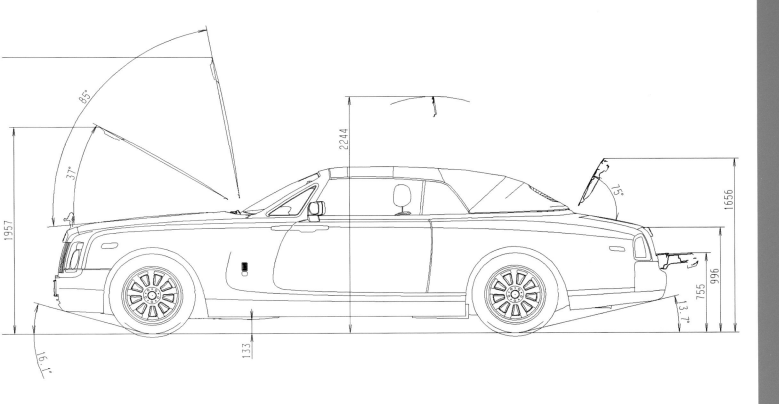

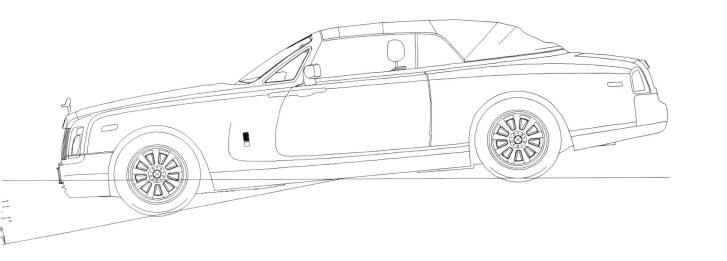

General arrangement
drawings define the
dimensions of the
Drophead Coupé and
reveal how accessible the
rear-hinged doors make
the car's interior.

Their travels took them to the Petersen Car Museum in Los Angeles, the Nethercutt Museum in San Sylmar and the Richard Carpenter Collection, situated next to DesignWorks USA in Newbury Park. The group immersed itself in the culture of the California convertible from the 1920s to the 1980s, viewing cars in both pristine condition and in need of restoration.

Stefan Conrady gave a presentation to all concerned on the top floor of the Petersen Museum, based on the design briefing produced by the original Working Group the previous year. Several of the many points raised are worth noting in order to understand the philosophy behind the launch of a convertible Rolls-Royce at the beginning of this new millennium.

The BMW Group is a master of brand placement, and it demands that a clear statement of a brand's parameters be identified. In the case of the Drophead Coupé, it was deemed desirable for it to build upon the following characteristics established for the Phantom:

Enduring – a classic modern exterior and interior theme.
Endeavour – pursuit of perfection, bold engineering, radical thinking and traditional craft values with a clean-sheet design, built at Goodwood.
Grace – expressed in interior and exterior attention to detail, a Rolls-Royce tone of voice (spoken softly, not shouted).
Presence – a unique statement through style of design and brand.

For the Drophead Coupé these qualities were defined in greater detail:

Enduring – the style must communicate that it is new but a credible development from the long line of Rolls-Royce cars that went before. It should be timeless but contemporary, avoiding fashion or gimmickry.
Endeavour – the style must communicate boldness and fresh thinking that is consistent with the strong original Rolls-Royce and Phantom heritage of engineering excellence.
Grace – the style must communicate the effortless elegance inherent in most earlier Rolls-Royce convertibles.
Presence – the execution of the above three should give a presence that is accessible and clear to all from connoisseur to the wider world.

Photos courtesy of the Petersen Automotive Museum

Opposite: in Los Angeles, the design team studied the Californian convertible culture, looking at classic American dropheads like this 1939 Plymouth DeLuxe. The fertile local environment has nurtured some of America's leading car designers.

Above: much favoured by members of Hollywood's 'Rat Pack', the limited-production Dual-Ghia was an intriguing blend of Italian style and American muscle, a 1960s Chrysler D-500 bodied in Turin for Detroit haulage contractor Gene Casaroll.

Above right: many lessons could be learnt from the ugly 1958 Edsel convertible, a misplaced marketing exercise by the Ford Motor Company. This legendary failure was one aspect of convertible culture that the Rolls-Royce team did well not to absorb!

Certain functional benefits were required of the design: uncompromised accommodation of four adults and their luggage, which might be three golf bags and related apparel; easy entry and exit, including to the rear passenger seating; 'snowbird compatibility' (appealing to the over-50s); and 'social functionality' (driver and passengers alike would share the delight of travelling in the car, making the journey a memorable occasion, not just a means of transport).

Seven challenges were identified for the Drophead Coupé: to build upon the success of the thirty-five year old Corniche; to retain the loyal customer base; to reach out to a broader market; to re-affirm the brand values manifested by the Phantom; to extend the core-positioning of the Phantom; to gain the pinnacle position in its class and to create a vision for Rolls-Royce Motor Cars.

All these would have to be met to realise four unique selling points for the Drophead Coupé. It would have to be the most emotional large car in the world; the most gorgeous car in the world; the most precious car in the world; and the most spacious four-seater convertible in the world.

Naturally, consideration was given to a pure Phantom convertible, a saloon with the top chopped off. Would it then retain four doors or be an extraordinary long two-door body? Discounting the engineering problems of torsional rigidity for a car of that length, the idea was rejected at the earliest viewing of the exterior design sketches. Even in shortened form, the car looked like the compromised creation that it would have been, and it was impossible to achieve the qualities and comply with the challenges that had been laid down for RR2.

One crucial decision had been made by the BMW Group during this time, which was to build a prototype of the proposed Drophead Coupé. Funds for such a project come from the BMW Group, not the BMW division. Marek Djordjevic elaborated. "The BMW Group normally reserves funds to build one concept car every year. There is a concept car Council, or show car Council,

within the BMW Group. It decides which concept cars the Group is going to build. Everybody has to present their case, and judgments are made on the thoughts and understanding of which brand is doing what at the time in question, and who will gain most from the Council's support. For 2003 it was agreed that Rolls-Royce had the strongest case, and so funds were allocated to produce '100EX'." Rightly, in line with 100 years of Rolls-Royce tradition, the car was neither called a show car nor a concept car; it is an 'Experimental Car'. And while show and concept cars are rarely fully operational road-going vehicles, '100EX' is fully functional in all aspects.

So, very early on, the concept of the Drophead Coupé became solid reality in the form of '100EX'. The approval it received went a long way to persuade the BMW Group board to give the go-ahead for a production Drophead Coupé.

Above and opposite above: taking the powertrain and spaceframe of the Phantom (above) as its starting point, the '100EX' Experimental car (opposite) was fully operational but very different in appearance from the saloon.

Opposite below: wherever '100EX' was exhibited, whether at motor shows or at selected dealerships, the public reaction was unanimous: 'It must go into production!'

Chapter Four
Adapting The Spaceframe

A key element in the successful business plan for the Drophead Coupé was the Phantom's spaceframe construction. The structure was chosen for the Phantom because of the relative ease with which a spaceframe can be altered by simply changing the dimensions of the various components. The designers knew that derivatives which could be assembled using the same production line would allow important financial and time-saving benefits. Most high-volume production cars use a semi-monocoque floor-pan and body-shell. The vehicle gains its strength from the sheet-metal pressings that are welded together. Alter the finished shell, and the strength of the whole unit might well be compromised.

A spaceframe gives the car load-bearing strength and the external panels just give the car its form. Spaceframe technology is rarely used in mass-produced vehicles, as it is relatively expensive to assemble. It is however much cheaper to develop a prototype spaceframe than a semi-monocoque. For a company the size of Rolls-Royce Motor Cars, with a very small number of cars produced, it is far better to save substantial amounts of money at the design stage, and only spend it as individual cars are built, with the ability to produce revenue soon after.

Opposite: the very strong spaceframe chassis originally created for the Phantom can easily be adapted to cater for variants of different dimensions, enabling them to share the same production line.

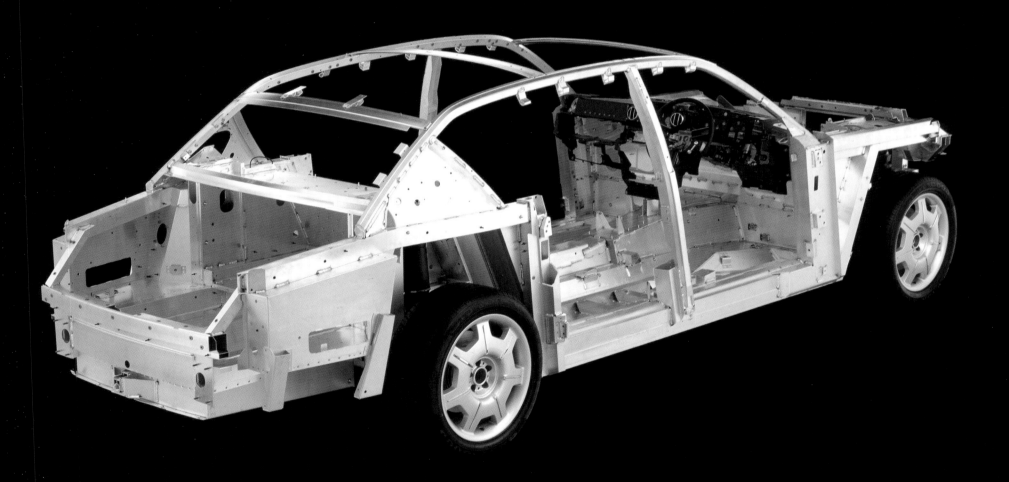

"There is no safe way of judging
anything except by experiment"
Sir Henry Royce

The Phantom and Drophead Coupé spaceframes consist of hollow extruded aluminium beams. By using aluminium instead of steel, a weight saving of twenty-five per cent is made, even though the actual walls of the aluminium extrusions are thicker to compensate for the lesser strength of aluminium. An impressive 2,535 separate welds covering 147 metres of welding seam, along with 358 self-piercing rivets, are used to assemble the extrusions and covering sheet-metal. Critical fixing points and surfaces are machined to 0.2mm accuracy and every dimension is checked by an automated measuring machine to ensure the complete spaceframe is built with total accuracy to a tolerance of less than half a millimetre.

Ian Robertson, chairman and chief executive of Rolls-Royce Motor Cars Ltd, is adamant about the commercial advantages of adapting an existing spaceframe: "The spaceframe gives you the flexibility to change the structure without going through all the engineering testing that would be needed if starting from scratch. You can alter and reinforce sections with relative ease, in our case building on knowledge that had already been acquired for the Phantom. I think we reduced our development time and development costs by thirty per cent each, against starting with a totally new structure."

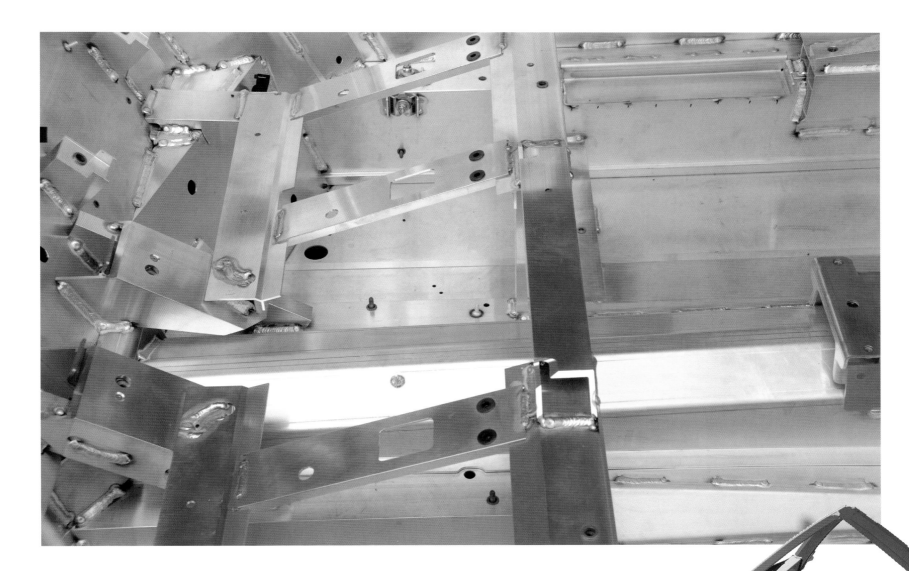

The roof of a closed car takes a lot of the torsional or twisting forces that occur when a car corners or when a wheel travels up and down on its suspension. Olaf Kraschienski, head of spaceframe design, had to ascertain where to add strength to the roofless spaceframe to compensate for this loss of rigidity. An obvious area was the floor-pan. Steel tension struts were added to the front and rear, along with the front shock absorber towers. The side sills were also increased in height, width and thickness. Kraschienski explained a necessary compromise. "The thickness of the extruded metal could ideally vary in any one section, but an extrusion can only be produced in a single chosen dimension, so there are areas which are by necessity over-engineered, although in terms of extra weight we are not talking of figures that will make a difference to the car's performance."

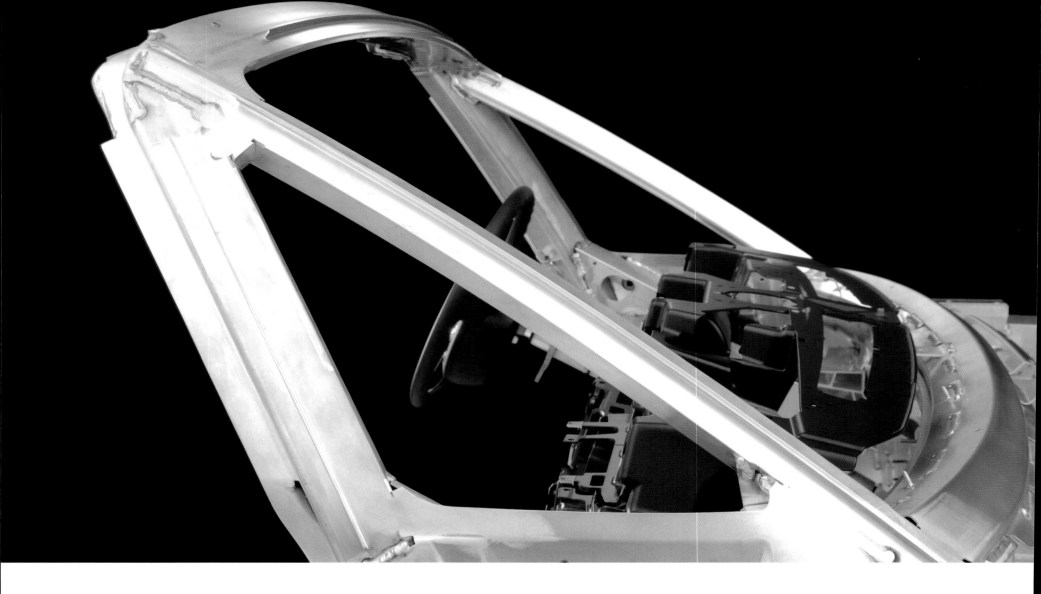

During the design team's visit to California, and following suggestions from chief designer Ian Cameron, chief engineer Karl Baumer had sketched a proposed triangulated windscreen and 'A pillar' for the car on a paper napkin while parked in a shopping mall near the Petersen Museum. By choosing a door that opened at the front, and a triangular 'A pillar' running from the windscreen right down to the floor pan, the door shut-line could run along an uncompromised 'A pillar unbroken by front-mounted hinge mechanisms. This would give immense rollover protection in the case of an accident, as well as enhanced torsional rigidity. Indeed, the Drophead Coupé has rollover protection virtually equal to that of the Phantom. At this ideas-only stage, no one realised just how effective this structure would be in virtually eliminating all scuttle-shake, the shimmying motion suffered by convertible cars on rough road surfaces. Baumer's design was of course based on sound engineering principles, but Ian Cameron's design team embraced the concept with open arms.

The Drophead Coupé has the same dimensions as the Phantom from radiator grille to windscreen, but is shorter overall. The reduced length makes the car more agile and responsive, and suits the chosen body styling. Apart from losing its roof, the greatest re-working of the spaceframe was at the rear to accommodate the hood and its mechanism. This meant that the fuel tank had to be re-shaped and reduced in capacity from 100 litres to 80 litres, so that the folded hood would be fully contained within the body profile.

Although not part of the actual spaceframe, the front wings attached to it are made by the Superform Aluminium Company of Worcester. The so-called 'super plastic forming' of aluminium is a production process widely used in the aircraft industry. A sheet of aluminium is heated to 470 degrees Celsius (878 degrees Fahrenheit), at which point it becomes almost liquid. In this plastic state, it is forced onto a single-surface form tool to create a complex three-dimensional shape. This is made possible by increasing the air pressure on the opposite side of the aluminium sheet, which pushes it on to the form tool. Shapes of far greater complexity and precision are achieved than by using a simple press tool. Using this method, the Drophead Coupé boasts the longest and most complex single-panel wings produced for the automotive industry.

For both the Phantom and the Drophead Coupé, this huge and very strong light-weight spaceframe is a major reason why both cars are capable of such impressive performance. In terms of straight line acceleration, the Phantom is, marginally slower, by a couple of tenths of a second to one hundred kilometers per hour or sixty miles per hour. This is due to more of the slightly greater weight of the Drophead Coupé resting on the rear wheels, a fact which aids acceleration. In the real world, where high average speeds are more important, the quicker responses of the Drophead Coupé, with its retuned suspension and shorter wheelbase, resulting in sharper handling, will have a distinct advantage over the saloon whether traversing the Italian Alps, the roads of Devonshire or the winding hills of Northern California.

Above: a huge benefit of spaceframe construction is the flexibility it gives to change the structure without having to start engineering testing all over again. Whole sections can safely be altered and reinforced by using knowledge already gained.

Opposite: while the Drophead Coupé has the same dimensions as the Phantom from radiator grille to windscreen, it is 9.5 inches /225mm shorter overall, requiring many changes in the construction of its spaceframe to compensate for the loss of the roof.

Chapter Five
Power To Spare

"Long rides of 200 miles or more in any Rolls-Royce refresh me more and leave me less tired than 100 miles in most other cars"
Country Life, 1906

The Drophead Coupé uses the same V12 cylinder engine as the Rolls-Royce Phantom, although the experimental '100EX' is powered by a one-off V16 engine designed by the BMW Group's head of engineering for special engines, Adolf Fischer, who adapted two V8 units to create it. Although quiet and powerful enough to be a Rolls-Royce power unit, the V16 offers no practical advantage over the Phantom's V12 engine, which develops all the power that the Drophead Coupé requires, without the extra cost and weight penalties of a car with a longer front end. There is not even an historic precedent for a production V16 cylinder Rolls-Royce engine. Happily the V12 engine and gearbox specifically designed for the Phantom needed no modifications to be transposed into the Drophead Coupé.

By the end of 2002, the V12 engines for the BMW 760 and the Rolls-Royce Phantom had been developed side by side. Components that were not specific to each vehicle could be produced together. This reduced development times and manufacturing costs. Without this symbiotic relationship, it is unlikely that BMW Group would have been able to make financial sense of buying Rolls-Royce. Project Rolls-Royce engineers worked on a dedicated production line at BMW's Munich engine facility. This allowed them as much close technical back up as they required for the development of the Phantom's engine but gave the promised autonomy. The normally-aspirated all-alloy 60 degree V12 had its bore and stroke increased to 92mm x 84.6mm to give the traditional Rolls-Royce capacity of 6.75 litres. Cylinder heads, inlet manifolds, pistons, connecting rods, crankshaft and the crankcase were some of the components specifically designed for the Phantom engine. It now required low speed torque that is the key to the magic 'waftability' – a term created a century ago by Rolls-Royce engineers after a writer in *The Autocar* described riding in the Rolls-Royce 40/50hp as 'being wafted through the countryside'. For the Phantom, this was achieved by designing the cylinder heads and inlet manifolds so that at a mere 1000rpm it developed seventy-five per cent of its maximum torque.

Developed alongside the BMW 760
engine, the Rolls-Royce V12 unit has so
many specifically designed components,
it can truthfully be described as a
different design.

Far left: the magic Rolls-Royce quality of 'waftability' was achieved by modifying the engine's cylinder heads and inlet manifolds to develop massive torque at low revolutions.

Left: Dr. Karlheinz Bierwirth, head of Project RR2 (left) discusses a styling issue from the engineers point of view with Dieter Budde, head of Rolls-Royce initial phase (middle) and Helmut Riedl, director of engineering (right).

But why was this so desirable? Dr. Tim Leverton, chief engineer for the Phantom's development, Project Rolls-Royce explained: 'The flatness of this curve is important through the engine speed range 1000-3000rpm, which is the typical engine speed range for normal city driving. Every time the driver depresses the throttle pedal the car picks up smoothly and without hesitation. This is the essential quality of 'waftability.' By contrast, with a turbocharged engine the driver has to wait until the engine has reached approximately 2000rpm before rocket propulsion kicks in. The absence of sufficient torque from rest demands a wider throttle opening to elicit a response, leading to the risk that to manoeuvre through busy traffic entails the engine continually moving up and down a much steeper torque curve. Potential for wheel spin at 80mph perhaps – but not waftability.'

Leverton recalled that the late Peter Baines, general secretary of the Rolls-Royce Enthusiasts' Club, had supplied him with the torque figures for the V12-engined Phantom III of the late 1930s: "We were a little surprised to see how much torque the Phantom III had. When calculated, it equated to an acceleration time of 6.3 seconds for 40 to 65 kph. Incidentally the Phantom and the Drophead Coupé complete the same manoeuvre in 2.2 seconds."

Consideration of emission control legislation and the engine's overall performance resulted in the use of a fuel injection system in which each cylinder has its own high pressure jet supplying a precisely measured amount of petrol directly into the combustion chamber. This evaporating spray of fuel has a cooling effect which allows a raised compression ratio of 11:1, which in turn produces higher thermal efficiency to give greater power and torque.

Camshaft timing can be varied by up to 60 degree crankshaft angle and is combined with a variable valve-lift mechanism. Control of the 48 valves precisely regulates the breathing throughout the rev range, maximising the engine's efficiency to reduce fuel consumption and help produce the desired torque curve. The fuel efficiency of the unit in this guise allied to the relatively low weight of the Drophead Coupé gives a combined fuel consumption of nearly eighteen miles per UK gallon. Rolls-Royce's customary admission of an 'adequate' power output is certainly still true. In the case of the Drophead Coupé, this coyness is replaced by the proud

statement that 453bhp has been achieved. On the road, this means that there is still approximately 90 per cent of power in reserve when cruising at the British legal limit of 70mph.

Once the carefully monitored and controlled fuel air mixture has done its job, it is expelled from the engine through a dual stainless steel exhaust system. Six silencers or 'resonators' expand and cool the spent gas on its way to the atmosphere. At any speed the resulting exhaust noise can only be called a gentle purr. For those occasions when an owner wishes to make an especially noise-free arrival or departure, a 'whisper valve' in each of the rear resonators of the exhaust system closes to allow near silent idling – subject of course to the depth of gravel beneath the tyres. During testing, it was found that when moving off slowly, with the hood down, a discernable 'click' could be heard when the 'whisper valves' open. The remedy was to alter their activation point to a higher engine speed, when tyre noise and airflow made the 'clicks' inaudible.

Above: for the new V12 power unit, bore and stroke dimensions were adopted to create an engine with a swept volume of 6.75 litres, a traditional Rolls-Royce capacity. Camshaft timing and valve lift are both variable, controlling the engine's 48 valves for maximum efficiency. The result is significant fuel efficiency and remarkable torque.

Power reaches the rear wheels via a six-speed ZF 6HP32 'shift by wire' automatic transmission electronically connected to the gear selector. There is a wide spread of ratios that give crisp acceleration and relaxed high-speed cruising. Upward shifts occur early and downward late. Although there is an emergency kickdown on the throttle pedal, the characteristically muscular torque means that a higher gear remains engaged longer than with other cars. Normal starts from rest are made in second gear, unless a rapid departure is sensed, in which case first is selected. There is also a 'low' button on the steering wheel, which enables a 'driver-selectable Low Programme' for use in mountainous terrain. The gearbox controller has adaptive control software which learns the driving style of the driver and appropriately alters the gear selection pattern.

During the testing programme it was found that the engine in its Phantom state of tune was also ideally suited to the Drophead Coupé. On first thoughts, this may seem strange as one is a formal saloon and the other a two-door four-seater with a more sporting demeanour. But when one considers that the Phantom weighs 2,550 kilograms and the Drophead Coupé is only slightly heavier at 2,620 kilograms, it makes more sense. Although the drophead is 70 kilograms heavier, the coefficient of drag is slightly less. The extra weight is due to the strengthening of the spaceframe, hood frame mechanism, and rollover protection system. The weight of the latter two is mainly over the rear wheels and assists the tyre grip under fast acceleration.

Whatever the shortcomings of Rolls-Royce models of the past, a bad engine has never been one of them. It is probable that when judged against such a standard of continued engineering excellence, motoring historians of the future will acknowledge this Rolls-Royce V12 engine as one of the great automotive engines of all time.

Below: the powertrain of the Drophead Coupé laid bare. A dual stainless steel exhaust system incorporating six silencers features 'whisper valves' that enable the car to arrive and depart in near silence.

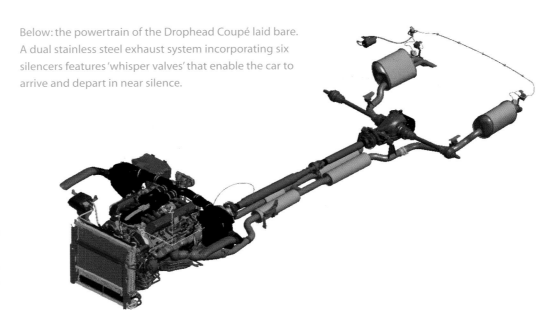

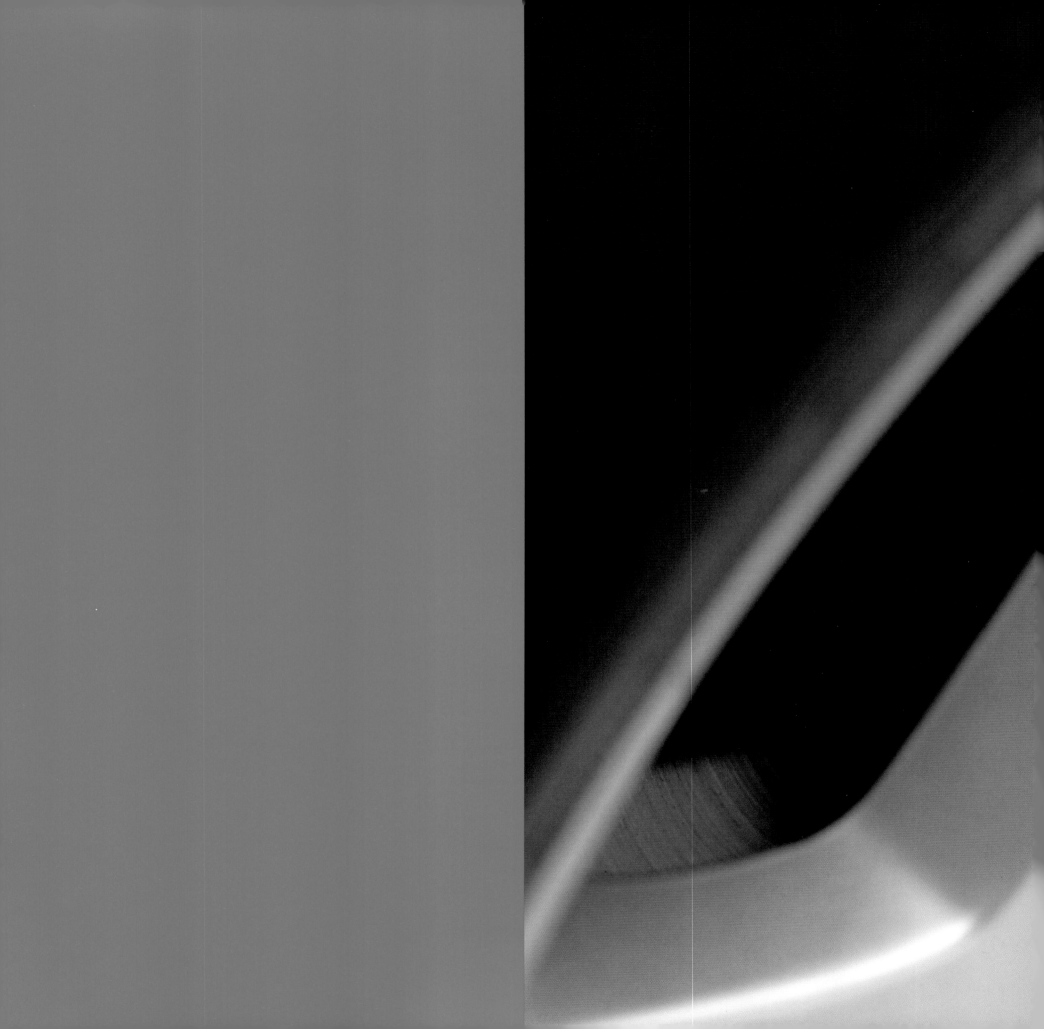

Chapter Six

From Wheel
To Wheels

For any vehicle to make the most of its suspension system, it needs as rigid a chassis/body structure as can be achieved. Otherwise a suspension set-up will be compromised by the flexing of a moving chassis. Just like the Phantom, the Drophead Coupé with its uniquely designed spaceframe structure comes close to being the perfect platform to which the suspension engineers can attach their hardware.

For the front suspension, a double wishbone arrangement with a tension link and lower control arm was chosen, giving a high degree of control over camber and track change over the whole range of movement and providing anti-dive characteristics under hard braking. There is even a hydraulic mount in the front suspension to damp out any vibration that could be transmitted to the steering wheel. The suspension is mounted on a tubular steel sub-frame for precise geometry, reduced noise and enhanced crash protection. The sub-frame itself is rigidly attached to the body at six points.

On the rear of the car the multi-link suspension is designed for ride comfort, preventing lift under braking forces and dive under acceleration. The rear sub-frame, made from 5mm thick hydroformed aluminium extrusions, is located on four large bushes that isolate chassis-borne noise and vibration from the rest of the car. The suspension links are also in aluminium, with the cast lower arms sitting parallel to the road in the normal position. They have an aerodynamic effect in smoothing the flow of air from the back of the moving vehicle. Front and rear anti-roll bars are mounted to the sub-frames with roller bearings for low friction and low noise.

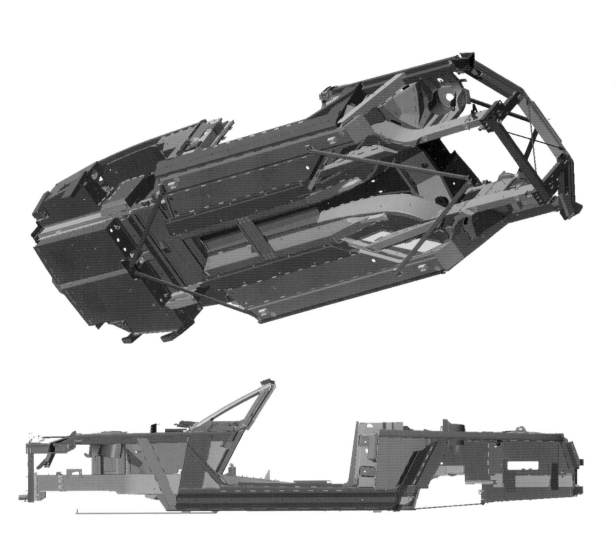

This page: where computer simulation was not that long ago confined to producing crude wire frame diagrams, now the entire structure of a car can be replicated in realistic detail and even crash-tested!

Opposite: the double wishbone front suspension, coupled with the combined air spring and shock absorber, gives a high degree of control over camber and track change, while keeping the car level under heavy braking.

> "When the engine is running, one can neither hear nor feel it"
> *'The Times' on the first Rolls-Royce, 1904*

Air springs are used all round for their ability to sustain constant soft spring rates and provide full spring travel regardless of load. So sensitive is the system that it can sense a rear-seat passenger moving across the car. The air springs can be raised up to one inch by the driver if conditions (such as rough ground) demand, and will automatically return to the lower position when the car reaches 40mph if the driver has forgotten to lower them.

The dampers on the Drophead Coupé's are electronically controlled: minimum damping for straight smooth roads, progressing to higher damping on corners and bumpy surfaces. By so doing, both passenger comfort and precise handling characteristics are achieved. The system monitors both the way the car is being driven and the road conditions up to one hundred times a second, or every twelve inches at 60mph.

The Drophead Coupé is 9.5 inches/225mm shorter than the Phantom, the centre of gravity is lower without the solid roof and the weight distribution is near 50/50 with the hood raised – all good points for the dynamics of a car that is more sporting in its driving manners.

However, Theo Martin, former head of Rolls-Royce Motor Cars testing, explained that the target was to tune the suspension to make the car the most comfortable open four-seater in the world, not the sportiest. "By tuning and retuning the damper settings in conjunction with differing diameters of anti-roll bars and spring rates, the optimum balance was found. An inherent problem when shortening the wheelbase of a car is the increased tendency for fore and aft pitching to occur. In the case of the Drophead Coupé, the combinations of all the various suspension settings made possible when using a really taut spaceframe allowed us to cancel out the inherent pitching tendency."

For the Drophead Coupé, the Rolls-Royce engineers have managed to retain the Phantom's ability to distance the driver and passengers from bad road surfaces and running over debris while still giving the driver that all-important feedback from the road surface that reveals what the wheels are doing. Theo Martin sums it up succinctly. "It's not like old American cars where you don't feel anything. It's a real rock-solid feeling and it gives you all the feedback you want, but it keeps you away from disturbances that you don't want."

Opposite above: beneath its elegant skin, the Drophead Coupé has a remarkably strong spaceframe, a near-perfect platform for the suspension engineers to attach their hardware.

Opposite below: though they share the same powertrain and similar spaceframes, the distinct differences between the Drophead Coupé and the Saloon are far more than skin deep.

Opposite: the gently swelling line of the Drophead body above the rear wheel arch, recalls the classic Corniche and gives the car a purposeful stance.

Above: when driving in a spirited fashion, the driver of a Drophead Coupé maintains mastery over the car thanks to the excellent body control.

When talking about a car's suspension, mentioning steering is unavoidable, as the one affects the other from the driver's perspective. If a car steers impeccably at slow and medium speeds, it might be slightly compromised at high speeds; the reverse effect is also true. There was some discussion concerning the speed at which the steering should feel best; at slow and medium speeds, or at high speeds above 100mph, the downside of the slower choice is that the steering response at speed would be 'sharper' and could have a marginal effect on the car's directional stability. Says Martin: 'The choice was made to trade off the potential for unimpeachable high-speed stability for more authoritive control at normal, every day driving speeds.'

So the driver of a Drophead Coupé, just like the Phantom driver, still experiences relatively direct steering, a primary ride that is just floating but not loose, and excellent body control so that when driving in a more spirited fashion, mastery will be maintained over the vehicle. In fact, although the variable-rate power assistance for the steering remains the same as the Phantom, the shorter wheelbase of the Drophead Coupé means that the car is more agile, reacting more sharply to changes of direction.

The design of the Drophead Coupé steering wheel with its large diameter rim of relatively thin section enhances the Rolls-Royce motoring experience. But it is not simply a matter of dimensions. In today's safety-conscious world that is governed by legislation, the wheel has to house an airbag and conform to many other safety requirements. In the case of the Phantom, the design called for the return of wheel-mounted controls that recall the Phantom III of the 1930s. All very costly to execute to the satisfaction of the safety testers, but the steering wheel is the most intimate bridge between driver and machine. If it looks or feels wrong, then the driving experience will be compromised.

Since the front section of the Drophead Coupé is based on the Phantom, it was no problem to keep the steering wheel position directly ahead of the driver. It is surprising how many cars today have wheel, driver's seat and pedals offset. It may not be significant on a short trip but it is slowly and relentlessly tiring on a long journey.

For the Phantom, Rolls-Royce Motor Cars decided to go against the fashionable trend for large diameter road-wheels with low profile tyres. This may be quite acceptable for sports cars and high performance versions of large saloons, but low profile tyres do compromise the ride quality. So the Phantom was planned to sit on large wheels with a lot of rubber around them – in fact, at 31 inches rolling diameter, the largest wheels fitted on any production passenger car today. Since the Drophead Coupé is designed to be a high-speed tourer and not an out-and-out sports car, the same Phantom range of wheels were chosen.

Chapter Seven
Beautiful To Behold

"I wanted to create a full four-seater convertible with two coach doors," says chief designer Ian Cameron, detailing his original vision for the Drophead Coupé. "My inspiration was for something less formal than the Phantom saloon and more performance orientated; something that would reveal the true dynamics and capabilities of the Phantom concept.

"My motivation was Sir Henry Royce's design for the experimental car '16EX', whose body was particularly light and aerodynamic for the 1920s. He built it to demonstrate that greater horsepower could be used to increase performance instead of allowing larger and heavier bodies to be fitted. Royce called the '16EX' 'a car with fizz', and I think this idea is dear to the heart of any driving enthusiast: to have a car capable of true performance."

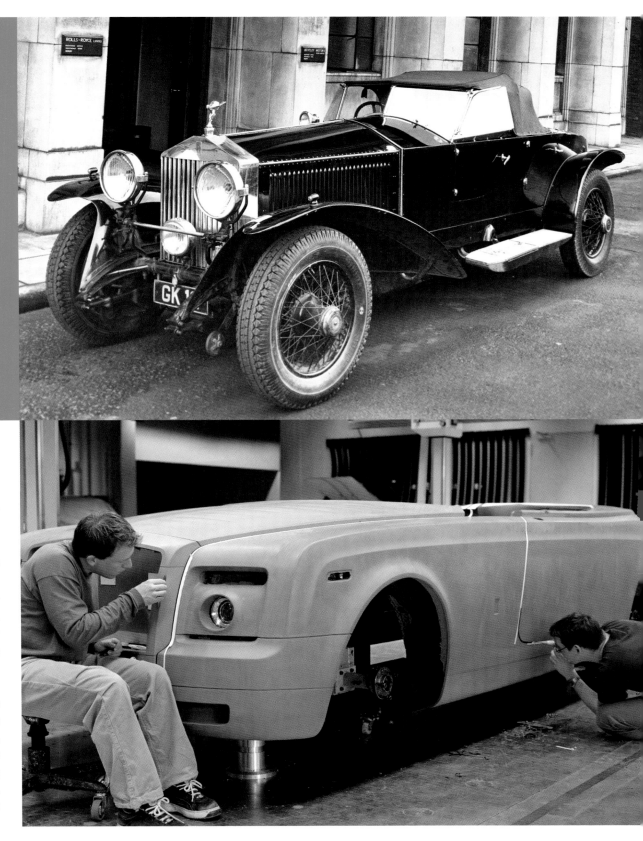

Opposite: a beautiful car in a beautiful setting, the Drophead Coupé pauses on California's coastal highway, one of the most scenic roads in North America.

Right: designer Ian Cameron's original vision for the Drophead Coupé was motivated by the sweeping shape of Sir Henry Royce's experimental car '16 EX' of the 1920s.

Below right: skilled modellers create the clay styling-buck for the body of the Drophead Coupé. Accurate in every detail, it would serve as the reference for building the real car.

Cameron gave a foretaste of the overall appearance of the Drophead Coupé in 2004, Rolls-Royce's centenary year, when he unveiled the very similar experimental car '100EX', which was "intended to give the impression of an elegant motor yacht at speed." Inevitably, there are differences between the two cars, ranging from minor items such as door-handle design to significant differences such as the replacement of the V16 engine of '100EX' with the Phantom saloon's V12 unit, yet overall they are so alike that to describe one is to describe the other.

The external appearance of the Phantom saloon was the work of Marek Djordjevic, who later performed the same task for both '100EX' and the Drophead Coupé. The initial design developed from discussions between Djordjevic and Cameron, with early ideas including an open four-door version of the saloon and a similar, but shortened, two-door version that still retained the saloon's front end.

These first ideas were perhaps obvious, as they represented the cheapest way of creating an open version of the Phantom saloon, but it was quickly realised that these options would create engineering difficulties or styling compromises – and the guiding principle behind the Drophead Coupé was that it was to be an uncompromised design.

Djordjevic summed up their underlying philosophy: "With the Phantom saloon, we had to re-establish the marque and retain its authenticity so that traditionalists would not be offended. With the Drophead Coupé we could afford to be more sporting and, like the historic Corniche, we suspected that it might well become a sub-brand in its own right, a car with its own enthusiastic following. Hence the dramatic streamlined form in the front, with the grille merging with the bonnet and wings far more than on any previous production Rolls-Royce. We were definitely not going to miss that chance to advance the aesthetic of the marque.

"Since this was to be a car of a more sporting nature, a slightly more aggressive look was appropriate, with slimmer sidelights above the round headlights. Then we could continue that sweptback gesture throughout the sides of the car."

A striking feature is the brushed stainless steel bonnet. While the bonnet of '100EX' had been formed from a single billet of aluminium, with a lattice girder reinforcement laser-cut into its underside for extra rigidity, this would have been prohibitively expensive for a production car. Moreover, it would have been virtually impossible to stop the aluminium from deteriorating in use without some kind of clear coating that would have compromised its appearance.

A basic concept of the Drophead Coupé was the use of materials that would complement each other, enhancing the visual appreciation of their different qualities. "Optical tactility" Cameron calls it. So while other metals were considered for the bonnet, stainless steel – the obvious choice – proved to be the best choice, because of its innate strength and corrosion resistance. It did not come without problems, for it was very difficult to achieve a uniform brushed finish over such a large area, and a suitable cleaner/polish had to be found to deal with finger marks and minor scratches. More importantly, a system for repair by local dealerships had to be devised should the bonnet suffer greater trauma.

Above left: a lesson from the past reshaped for the future, the decision to use a natural metal finish on the bonnet of the Drophead Coupé was inspired by the unpainted aluminium bonnets fitted to some early Silver Ghosts.

Above right: the eye is tricked into believing that the Drophead Coupé's bonnet seems longer by making the rear windscreen pillar wider than the front pillar.

Opposite: an unusual angle on the classic beauty of the Drophead Coupé.

During the development of the basic design, Djordjevic had the worry of not knowing whether these problems could be solved, and so he perfected his design to allow for either bare stainless steel or a painted bonnet. So successful was he that Rolls-Royce decision makers have allowed the option of stainless steel or painted bonnets, whichever the customer chooses.

The windscreen and quarter-light surround are instantly noticeable. Made from stainless steel, this component forms part of the spaceframe, giving the Drophead Coupé unparalleled rollover protection for an open car. Though it was originally devised as a styling feature, the engineers instantly became aware of its tremendous safety advantages and its ability to enhance the torsional rigidity of the entire car. It is a prime example of the old engineering adage, "if it looks right, it is right"!

Marek Djordjevic sums it up: "It's the essence of what Rolls-Royce is all about. It's the result of taking the right decisions for the right reasons. Every line and feature of the saloon and the Drophead Coupé is there for more than one reason."

While '100EX' had a longer front end than the Drophead Coupé, since it was fitted with a one-off V16 engine rather than using the saloon's V12 power unit, Djordjevic wanted to retain the visual balance of '100EX' as much as possible, and by a slight change to the windscreen form, the eye can be tricked into believing that the car's proportions are similar. The experimental car has the wider screen pillar at the front, while the wider pillar is at the rear on the production car, making the bonnet appear longer than it really is.

The use of brushed stainless steel, though as trim rather than structure, is continued around the entire passenger compartment of the car. This, when combined with the teak-wood cover that conceals the folded hood, reveals the strong nautical influence on the coachwork.

Above: the designers took care to give the Drophead Coupé a distinctive personality with strong sporting overtones.

Opposite: the timeless styling of the Drophead Coupé blends perfectly with any style of architecture. The car is seen here at the Quintessa Winery, Napa Valley, California.

Above left: as a prelude to production, the split boot lid was modelled full-size in clay and then covered in a plastic film called Di-Noc that gives the impression of a painted metal surface.

Below left: carried over from Experimental Car '100EX' is the ingenious split luggage-boot lid whose horizontal upper part lifts in the normal way, but has a vertical lower section that drops down like a tailgate.

Above right: closed, the boot of the Drophead Coupé does not reveal its split personality.

Below right: memories of picnics at Royal Ascot and American tailgate parties before football games, inspired chief stylist exterior design, Marek Djordjevic to create a drop-down tailgate strong enough to comfortably support the weight of two adults.

Bathed in the soft glow of a California sunrise that perfectly picks up the bright accent line running from stem to stern, the Drophead Coupé proudly displays the perfect lines of its beautifully crafted cloth soft-top. Five layers of material insulate the occupants from the soft morning mist sweeping in from the Pacific Ocean.

An ingenious feature of '100EX' was a split luggage-boot lid whose horizontal upper part lifted in the normal way, but the vertical lower section dropped down like a tailgate. It was Marek Djordjevic's idea. "I remember our trip to Royal Ascot and how wonderful it was to see the people enjoying picnics next to their cars. Then I thought of the tailgate parties that Americans have in the parking lots before a football game, and my younger days visiting crowded cafés in Europe or Los Angeles, thinking how much better it would be to park my car right outside and enjoy the coffee and food as I watched the world go by. Obviously that's not the intended use for the Drophead Coupé, but these were all seeds from which the idea grew."

An eye-catching styling exercise, the split luggage-boot lid worked admirably and soon became one of the most admired features of the experimental car. Somehow, it was going to have to be included in the production car, whose tailgate is strong enough to provide comfortable "picnic" seating for two adults.

A crucial feature of any drophead coupé is of course its hood. Nowadays, many designers of convertible cars opt for a retractable hard-top, but this was rejected for several reasons for the Drophead Coupé, whose fabric hood – the largest of any modern convertible car – uses five layers of material to insulate the interior. Much more space is needed to stow a metal top, and when raised, it gives no real feeling of being in a convertible. It is a compromise. A raised soft-top looks intriguing.

Drophead Coupé owners will have several cars in their garages and they will choose the right car for the occasion. As Ian Cameron puts it, "They don't want a reversible jacket, they want the real thing."

There is also what can only be called the romantic element in a beautifully crafted cloth soft-top, especially on a rainy night, when the whole interior of the car becomes cosier. The soft sound of raindrops on the cloth is relaxing at the very least, and at best can be as romantic as a dozen red roses lying next to a bottle of iced champagne, if the right passenger is with you.

Chapter Eight

From The
Inside Out

Looks may not be everything, but they do play a crucial role in the choice of a car. Its exterior coachwork may attract a prospective buyer and its performance will reinforce that attraction, but the interior will clinch the deal, for that is where the customer will enjoy the driving experience and the passengers will most appreciate the choice of car.

An added factor in the design of a convertible's interior is that it must harmonise with the exterior, for with the top down both aspects of the car's design will be seen at the same time. If conflicting themes are used, the car will just not look or feel right.

Ian Cameron was aware that Charles Coldham, who had been the chief interior designer for the Phantom saloon, had been musing over designs for a drophead coupé, should one ever be considered by Rolls-Royce. Following the success of his Phantom saloon interior, he was the obvious choice to take a similar role on the RR2 project.

Alan Sheppard had also worked on the Phantom saloon interior, and once Coldham had come up with his conceptual designs, Sheppard brought those ideas into reality, working with the design and production engineers: "Charles has to be liberal in his thinking, whereas I have to deliver the goods."

Above: no pleats interrupt the smooth leather surfaces of the seats and interior trim.

Opposite above: interior design leader Alan Sheppard (left) discusses a styling detail on a prototype mock-up with interior designer Charles Coldham (right).

Opposite below: designed for socialising, the 'lounge' rear seat of the Drophead Coupé is strictly intended as a private space for two.

110

Charles Coldham remembered the early days. "The nautical concept was Ian Cameron's. He wanted something that expressed the more relaxed, more recreational bias for which this car was going to be used. We wanted the Drophead Coupé to be more of a social animal than a Ferrari or a Maserati, or any of the out-and-out performance cars. Our car needed to be for socialising and sharing with other people. The journey should be as pleasing as the destination, not just for the driver, but for the passengers as well."

Left: to ensure the upholstery has a smooth, unblemished surface, every hide is inspected for the slightest flaw before cutting begins so that the most efficient use can be made of the leather.

Opposite: the commanding view from the driver's seat. The analogue instruments whose classic dials display easily interpreted information on the Drophead Coupé's performance are framed in a machined metal panel.

Typical of this rationale is the Drophead Coupé's 'lounge' rear seat, which is perceived as more intimate than individual seats. From the beginning, the rear seat was always going to be for two occupants, not three. Vertical storage cabinets in the footwell ahead of the rear-seat arm-rests enhanced the feeling of a private space for the rear passengers. As well as creating an intimate space, this allowed room at the sides for the hood mechanism; providing three rear seats would have compromised the occupants' comfort.

Front seat occupants are cosseted in lightweight sporting seats with more than a passing resemblance to the bucket seats of the iconic Bentley R Type Continental built by Rolls-Royce in the early 1950s. Although looking lighter in construction than those of the Phantom saloon, the Coupé's seats are, in the writer's opinion, more comfortable, although the seat cushions could perhaps be extended further forward to give greater leg support. The leather upholstery is of equal quality to that used in the saloon, and perfectly capable of standing up to the rigors of dust and rain. The whole hide is dyed right through in a drum-pigmentation process, not just surface-coloured, which also helps resistance to wear and tear. This, despite the skins being equal in softness to the finest hides used in the clothing industry.

There are no pleats on the seats and interior trim, the leather surfaces reminding one of the upholstery of fashionable high quality cars of the 1930s. On a practical note, the materials used for the interior trim – leather, wood and carpet – are all water resistant; it is easier to brush rain-drops from a smooth leather surface than one that is stitched and pleated.

Ahead of the driver is a fascia identical to that of the saloon except for its upper section which, in place of wood veneers, has all-metal panels decorated with diagonally-machined, book-matched (or mirror-image) surfaces converging on the centre of the car.

This look is felt to be more in keeping with the informality of the car; it also provides a bridge between the exterior and interior styling elements. The lower part of the fascia and the other interior wood surfaces in the Drophead Coupé can be finished to the customer's choice in mahogany, rosewood, oak, elm cluster, ash burr or piano black. All the wood trim is sourced from sustainable, managed forests, where the chosen trees are reaching the end of their life spans.

As Alan Sheppard is keen to emphasise that while all the launch cars have the teak wood option, it is not compulsory. One might suspect that the mixture of matt teak on the door fillets and high-gloss wood on the fascia might jar, but that is not the case. Charles Coldham was insistent that the teak should continue along the sides and door-tops from the rear decking, with a cut-away for the door-pulls, which are framed by polished chromium surrounds that flare slightly to define and highlight them. Coldham was most certainly right to stand his ground.

In the manner of classic skiff coachwork, experimental car '100EX' featured a teak wood floor with caulked separations that matched the rear decking. Eye-catching as it is, this finish proved to be unsuitable for a modern production car, as Alan Sheppard explains: "Wood floors get pretty slippery when wet, and can be a real nuisance for ladies in high-heeled shoes. So we chose a synthetic sisal material for the foot mats that is mould resistant in the high temperature, high humidity environments that many of these cars will experience."

The nautical influence defining the Drophead Coupé's passenger compartment is evident. Chief designer Ian Cameron evoked the design and finish of 1930s racing yachts and Italian Riva speedboats.

Above: the lucky owner might be pulling away from yacht club or golf club, restaurant or church. Wherever the car is, a last look as it leaves is enough to make anyone envious.

Right: attention to detail is evident everywhere in the Drophead Coupé, right down to the use of retro tonneau fasteners to retain the weather-resistant sisal carpet.

For the same reasons, the carpet throughout the Drophead Coupé is man-made. The traditional wool or wool-and-jute mixture could harbour dampness and be prone to unpleasant odours caused by mould. It is virtually impossible to tell that the carpet material specified is not 100 per cent wool, in either its look or feel. However, it was possible to use the traditional cashmere headlining material for the hood. Being in a part of the car where any relative dampness will only be the result of high humidity, it will spend much of its time dry enough to withstand the onslaught of mould spores. The cashmere chosen, with its feel of unequalled opulence, is the most luxurious headlining in any production convertible.

In terms that satisfy both aesthetics and practicality, the designers paid as much attention to minor details as they did to the overall concept. For instance, the levers that enable the front seat-backs to pivot forward are finished in satin-chromium plating and shaped to feel just right to the human hand, a quality that Rolls-Royce has applied to control handles, levers and switches for many years.

A stylish and useful feature on the Phantom saloon is the inclusion of an umbrella concealed in each rear door edge. The Drophead Coupé repeats this attribute, but here they are housed in the rear edge of the front wings, access is again possible when a door is open.

Wide open and inviting, the rear-hinged door of the Drophead Coupé gives easy access to the welcoming rear compartment. Natural materials – wood and leather – are employed to the best advantage.

Above left: the levers that allow the backs of the front seats to pivot forwards are carefully shaped to fit the human hand, a logical principle that Rolls-Royce has followed for years.

Above right: the beautifully crafted handle of one of the front-wing mounted umbrellas can only be seen with the door open. A casual passer-by would be hard pressed to guess what the handle might be attached to. Easily withdrawn from its front-wing storage space, one of the tightly rolled Teflon-coated umbrellas can be protecting driver and passengers in only a few seconds. Owing to its Teflon coating, it may be replaced whilst still damp, without any worries about deterioration of the fabric.

The rear compartment ashtrays, capable of dealing with the biggest cigars that Havana can offer, are large and impressive, with a distinct Art Deco look. Indeed, if you had to append a design style to the interior of the Drophead Coupé, then the "automobile-chic" Art Deco illustrations of the exotic 1920s high society artist Tamara de Lempicka might spring to mind. But to hint at such retro-styling would be unfair to Coldham, as his work is very much of today. His remit was to interpret the design of past great Rolls-Royce drophead coupés, with the use of traditional materials where possible, but in a style that is completely suited to the third millennium. He has entirely succeeded in this task, and in so doing has been able to convey the intended sense of excitement and romance.

Driver and passengers alike will enjoy the tactile and visual expression of sheer voluptuousness that balances the sporting attributes of the car, a combination rarely found in automobiles of today.

The Phantom Drophead Coupé shows
off its complex and attractive hood
outside the Goodwood Head offices of
Rolls-Royce Motor Cars Ltd, just a few
yards from the manufacturing plant.
Inside can be seen a pair of Phantom
saloons, and the side view of a Drophead
Coupé spaceframe, all being admired by
a portrait of Sir Henry Royce.

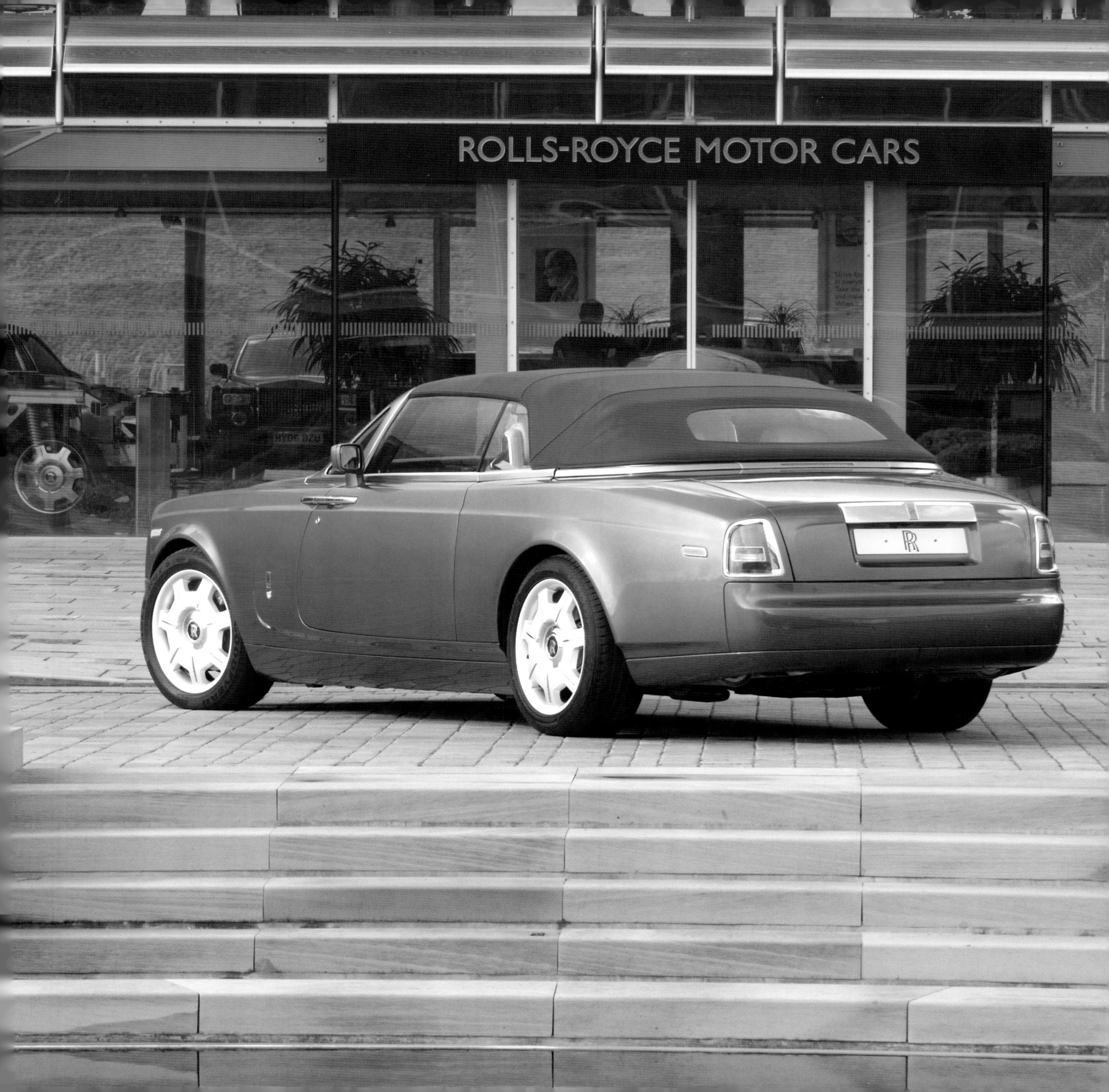
ROLLS-ROYCE MOTOR CARS

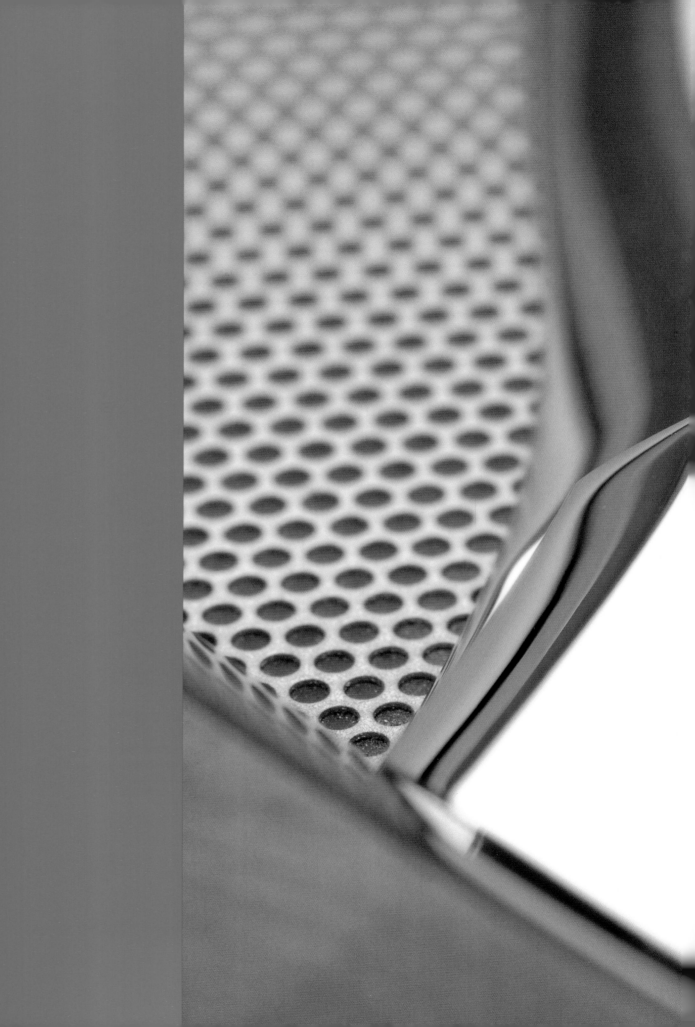

Chapter Nine
Colour, Conformity And Custom-Built

Sami Coultas might have been the youngest team member on Project RR2, but on her shoulders rested one of the greatest influences on the customer's decision-making process; she was responsible for the choice of colours used throughout the Drophead Coupé. Once Ian Cameron had agreed the designs submitted by Charles Coldham and Alan Sheppard, it was all up to Sami Coultas.

She explains the process: "A colour and trim designer puts together colour and material combinations based on experience with existing customers, knowledge of available elements, and visits to shows and shops that are relevant. Textile exhibitions, furniture and boat shows, antique shops and historic buildings, like Italy's Villa d'Este – these are the sort of places I visited."

Coultas started her programme by reviewing information supplied by the sales team about the probable customer base. Like everyone involved with the RR2 project, she was urged to view the car as being more sporting and less conservative than the Phantom saloon.

Early ideas were distilled into three themes: 'Maritime' – which replicates the style of '100EX' – 'Town', for the city sophisticate, and 'Country', with the latter themes scheduled to become available after the initial launch period of the car. While the final choice of colour and textures will always rest with the customer, Coultas must make sure that those selected do not conflict with one another within those themes. "I start with the exterior paint colours, of which there were nine for the launch of the Drophead Coupé. The Xirallic metallic paint used contains small amounts of pigments that cause a sparkle, tinged red or green depending on the light. It is a very subtle finish compared with the silver of a traditional metallic paint."

The next surface to consider was the hood material, a twill cloth: one of the six colours offered is a high-tech weave containing metallic threads. Factors that had to be considered included fading, water repellence, creasing, cleaning ability and general wear and tear. Some colours proved better than others.

Choices for interior coverings, hood lining, door trim, carpets and seats followed; all needed to be as tolerant as the hood material, but with the added consideration that they are subject to more intense wear. Three interior combinations are available; 'Standard', with a vertical theme which contains contrasting elements, 'Mono', with minimum contrast within one colour theme, and 'Linear', with a horizontal or marine-derived theme much inspired by Riva boats. The leather will be available in eleven colours by the end of the first year of production; carpets match or contrast as the customer chooses.

Different colour combinations are favoured in different world-markets. Coultas would have liked to visit individual countries to use the local light when making her choices, but this was not financially viable. However, she does work with natural daylight, avoiding the use of deceptive computer-generated mock-ups. "I use my expertise and experience of different parts of the world to make up the colour palettes. I am lucky in that my eye has a good memory."

Working closely with Sami Coultas, Charles Coldham, and especially Alan Sheppard, was Kris Sukhu, who bears the impressive title of surface integration manager. His work started when each visible component of the car was given a surface treatment, such as dye for leather on the seats, a paint finish on the exterior coachwork or a chromium-plate finish on a door handle. Sukhu explains the division of labour. "Charles and Alan devise the form that a component shall have and Sami chooses the colours and the compatibility with that of other components. I then develop the feel and the look of the component, the softness of the leather or the amount of sheen that a brushed metal part might have. We devise master panels for colours and finishes." Records of their decisions are kept in a three-hundred page book which identifies all the different surface treatments.

Most of Sukhu's work is spent on interior components, for the simple reason that there are many more of them than there are exterior details, although the stainless steel bonnet proved time-consuming.

Above left: Alan Sheppard and Sami Coultas contrast samples of hard and soft trim for the Drophead Coupé.

Above right: choosing interior coverings for the new car. Materials not only must be colour fast but also be resistant to intense wear. Factors that must be considered include fading, water repellence and creasing.

Opposite: built for the outdoor life, the Drophead Coupé features interior trim that has proved its ability to withstand exposure to the elements.

Sukhu reminisced. "There were about fifteen people working on getting the bonnet right. We found an old DeLorean, from around 1980, with its entirely unpainted stainless steel bodywork, resting on a farm in Germany, which the farmer allowed us to take to Munich. We learnt quite a lot about what to do and what not to do for finishes on stainless steel. Not only did we have to get the sheen just right to be attractive, to lose some of the natural yellow colour of the material and to minimise sun-glare, but we had to come up with something that was economically repairable in service, should it be damaged. That was probably my biggest single challenge on the Drophead Coupé."

But what became of the friendly farmer's DeLorean? It seems that it was driven back to him, not completely renovated, but well refurbished and ready for use.

Once Sukhu had established the finish for a component, he had to be assured that individual suppliers and contractors could meet those very stringent demands. He continues: "It is quite possible that one supplier will provide us with, say, a brushed-chromium-plated component that will sit next to another one from a totally different manufacturer. I have to make sure both contractors can repeatedly supply the same finish; and the same goes for dyed leather, paint or anything else."

Another layer of responsibility for just how a completed car looks falls on Goodwood's Bespoke department. Headed by Clive Woolmer, this is the department that creates and builds any special features requested by a customer, including non-standard materials, finishes and colours. There will always be people who would like their cars to be that little bit special, or may have exacting needs because of a particular use for which the car might be destined.

The outstanding example of the Bespoke service must be the fourteen identical Phantom extended wheelbase cars delivered to the Peninsula Hotel of Hong Kong. A long-time owner of a fleet of chauffeur driven Rolls-Royce cars, the hotel required thirty-nine changes to be made to the standard production cars. These ranged from the inclusion of disposal containers in the rear door-pockets for cold towels taken from the rear passenger-compartment's refrigerator to moving the climate controls from the centre console to each rear door and increasing the luggage boot space by re-siting a battery and the suspension's air-spring compressor.

The Peninsula Hotel's owner, Sir Michael Kadoorie, oversaw the cars' modifications; more a pleasure than a chore for Sir Michael, as he is a truly enthusiastic collector of classic Rolls-Royce cars. He commented at the handover ceremony when the cars were delivered to the hotel: "Rarely are my expectations exceeded, but on this occasion they have been. The cars, like the hotel, must exemplify quality, and the service requirements have also mirrored these high standards." Praise indeed from one of the world's foremost hoteliers!

Woolmer expects that most requests for changes to the Drophead Coupé will be less demanding. These might be for different paint, hood and leather colours, the addition of monograms or the interlinked 'R-R' letters of the Rolls-Royce logo on door cappings or stitched into head-rests or seat-backs. Of course, a family crest discreetly emblazoned on the outside of the doors would be no trouble at all.

The rear-compartment side storage-bins are capable of containing any bespoke feature that their dimensions permit. Something associated with social drinking is an expected favourite, whether it is cut crystal glass or the accompanying bottles of the passengers' chosen refreshment.

Woolmer would prefer that customers choosing a refrigerator are happy for it to be in the boot, especially with the picnic boot-lid. He enthuses: "I can imagine the owner and his friends sitting around the rear of the car at an event such as the English Derby horse race or Henley Regatta, enjoying cold Champagne and lunch from a beautifully made picnic set. I anticipate creating cars with really special 'wow factors' for specific events."

The decking of classic sailing yachts was the inspiration for the rear decking of the Drophead Coupé, echoing a fashion of the vintage years when skiff-bodied cars were all the rage.

Admiral Blue

Diamond Black

Duck Egg Blue

Any colour you like… the palette from which the owner of a Drophead Coupé may choose is limitless; if the standard palette of nine colours does not fit the customer's fancy, Goodwood's paint facility can create literally thousands of shades to order.

The Bespoke department does not have the vast resources of the original development and testing programme for the car, and so bespoke components are more likely to be over-engineered than stressed to the last degree. Woolmer explains. "For instance, when you look at the option of a bespoke cup-holder, it's a beautifully-engineered piece of polished aluminium weighing several kilos. It's a fantastic piece of work, very expensive, like jewellery; it's still a cup-holder, but a cup-holder with real style."

On occasion, bespoke features will find their way on to production cars, when an idea proves particularly attractive or just plain sensible. This might well be the case when a celebration run of cars is built, such as the Phantom Black saloon, a special edition proposed by Coultas and Sukhu. They approached Woolmer with an achievable concept, and he brought it to fruition.

Woolmer comments on the Phantom Black: "By selecting black ash-wood, a black metal fascia, black interior and exterior, finished off by the addition of exposed tailpipes, we created a whole new personality for the Phantom saloon. It was very exciting to work on a project that showed the Phantom could be something different."

As with all stages of the Drophead Coupé development and manufacture, the finishes on the car are the result of teamwork. While that may be true for virtually any motor vehicle built today, what sets the Rolls-Royce Motor Cars team-members apart is their enthusiasm for their work and their pride in the finished product. It is impossible not to be aware of this, especially if you are a customer choosing the colour, trim and bespoke features for your own car; that is the time at which the future owner becomes an associate member of the Rolls-Royce Motor Cars team, even if it is only for a few hours.

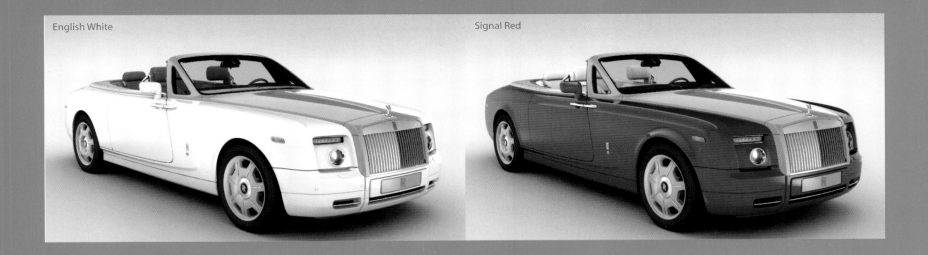

English White

Signal Red

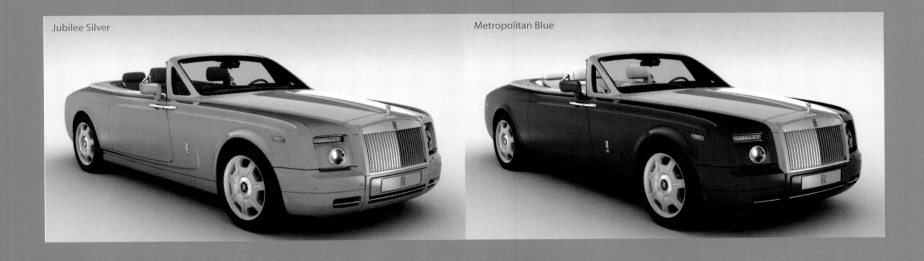

Jubilee Silver

Metropolitan Blue

Semaphore Yellow

Woodland Green

Chapter Ten
Testing
Times

"Royce was the only man to put
heart into an automobile"
Henry Ford

The Phantom test programme was completed in the unbelievably short period of 34 months, and for the Drophead Coupé time was once again limited, but since much of the work done for the Phantom would apply, the Drophead Coupé test programme would be correspondingly shorter. However, it was not simply a matter of fulfilling legal requirements and ticking boxes on test documents, for a car with an altered wheelbase and no roof structure might well reveal unforeseen problems on the road.

Computer-simulated testing at the design stage saved time and money as the re-configured spaceframe took shape. The engineers were able to produce an open-topped car of unmatched rigidity fitted with the Phantom's air springs, shock absorbers and stabiliser bars. These three components can be altered to give the best settings for the required handling and ride characteristics, and it is the testers' ability to sense what is required and relay the information to the engineers that enables the desired result to be achieved.

Above: during its Alpine cold weather trials, a pre-production car demonstrates the thermal efficiency of the hood materials, as the fallen snow clings resolutely to the cloth. Meanwhile the electrically heated glass rear window has efficiently cleared.

Opposite: computer-generated images of the body structure are so accurate that they can be used in simulated crash tests, sparing costly prototypes from destruction during the development programme.

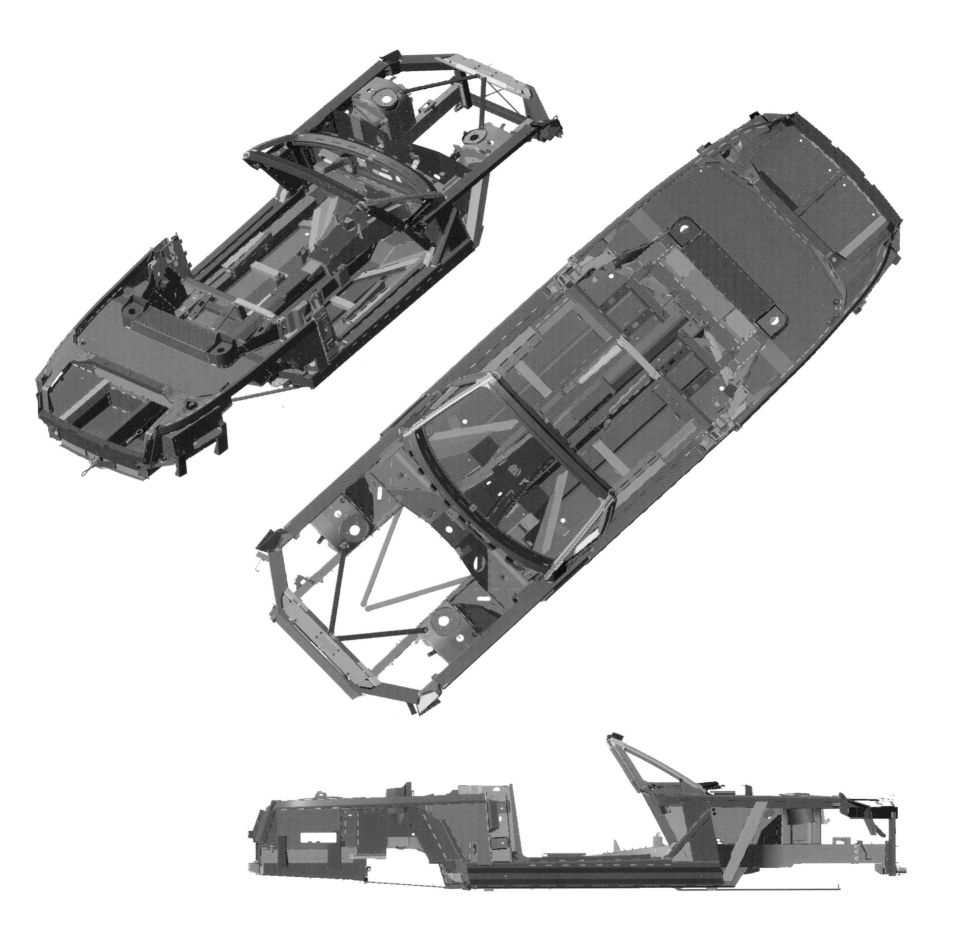

And so it was in this case, for the shortened wheelbase and revised suspension ratings made the Drophead Coupé feel more responsive and more agile than the Phantom. In terms of pure handling response, the test drivers could have asked for a lighter, aluminium bonnet so that the reduced weight over the front wheels would have allowed an even more responsive handling set up. But that would have adversely affected the ride, compromising the design imperative of being the world's most comfortable open four-seater car. The stainless steel bonnet stayed.

These pages: winter testing in the Austrian Tyrol took place around the ski resort of Hochgürgl, where mountain roads zigzag crazily upwards towards the nearby Italian frontier, testing the cold climate abilities of the Drophead Coupé to the full. The car performed outstandingly on the frozen mountain roads, thanks to its Dynamic Traction Control's ability to counter wheelspin on slippery surfaces.

Far away from the prying lenses of press photographers, the new Rolls-Royce proved itself on icy roads in sub-zero temperatures. Security was provided by a friendly farmer who allowed the prototypes to be hidden behind his stables.

Road-testing is not only about a car's performance. Every small detail must be checked, and in the case of Rolls-Royce, some 160 record books must be completed itemising every detail of each test. These include checks and reports on everything from air conditioning control dial tension through windscreen washer spread and annunciator light brightness to the feel of the window-winder button – literally hundreds of items and systems. If a problem is found, it is reported by the tester directly to the engineers concerned, including photographs, and as often as possible whilst examining the car that is faulty. They will redesign or adapt the part in question and it will be refitted to a test car. At some stage of the test programme it will be re-allocated to the car on which it first failed, to make sure there is no 'knock-on effect' caused by other components.

The Drophead Coupé test programme was undertaken in six countries. The first three cars, having been built at the BMW Group engineering and development facility, were driven in Munich city traffic and also at the BMW Group test track at Aschheim. Siegfried Wesinger was group leader of one of the test teams. He explained what happened during those first tests. "We have a lot of driving programmes. The professional test-drivers drive the cars non-stop in two shifts. At the end of each shift, they report to the engineers and download the car-borne computers relevant to the tests. The Munich runs are about 60 per cent autobahn driving, 30 per cent urban and rural roads, and 10 per cent other roads. Each durability test runs for 30,000 kilometres, which is equivalent to 150,000 kilometres of normal use by an owner. The Munich tests are the shakedown for the main components that might need attention, without the car being too far away from the engineering departments, should they be needed."

Above: a deserted road in South Africa's Northern Cape Province, the venue for intensive testing of engine sensors, steering and brake components.

Opposite: it's unlikely that any Drophead Coupé owner will wish to drive through floods as a matter of course, but it's reassuring to know that the ability is there should the emergency arise.

This page: cleared for high-speed testing by the South African police, this Drophead Coupé traversed desert roads at top speed when it was safe to do so. At times, the temperatures were so high that the surface of the bonnet reached a searing 80 degrees Celsius (176 degrees Fahrenheit).

Opposite: testing on the poorly-surfaced roads of South Africa revealed how components like the hood fabric performed in high temperatures and dusty conditions. Typical durability test runs averaged 30,000 kilometres.

Next, the cars were sent to South Africa, where extended high-speed runs could be carried out on occasionally rutted, always dusty and sometimes gravel-strewn roads. With the agreement of the South African Government, the testers were allowed to ignore speed restrictions, if deemed safe to do so. Helmut Riedl, director of engineering Rolls-Royce Motor Cars, was one of the first to drive the Drophead Coupé there. His comment "When I drove it the first time a long way in South Africa, I was happy, absolutely happy, everyone was happy. Wow! What a completely different experience with this car compared to other convertibles."

Siegfried Wesinger elaborated, "We did over 1,500 kilometres on the worst of the dust roads, one reason being to see how the hood would take the punishment, both up and folded into its compartment. We found the lighter coloured cloths, such as fawn, were prone to discolouration. It turned out to be a dye problem rather than the material itself. The way the hood folded needed to be changed in order to stop chafing if folded down with dust on it. In the hot South African sun, there was also a problem with an adhesive used around the hood's rear window. It was easily corrected with a more heat-resistant glue."

Left: the South African tests revealed a potential problem when the adhesive used to retain the rear window failed to stand up to the high temperatures. The problem was easily corrected with glue with greater heat resistance.

Below left: looking more suited to arctic weather than the South African sun, two Husky dogs guard the Drophead Coupé during a pause in its exhaustive testing programme.

Note was also taken of how the dust flowed across the contours of the body and how much of it settled on the car's upholstery. In both cases the team working on the computer-aided design phase of development had done a good job, and what little dust did settle on the seats proved to be easily removable. A more difficult problem was encountered at high-speed with the top up, especially when passing large trucks. The side windows were pulled outward by the low-pressure air, a similar effect to the top-surface of an aircraft wing as it creates lift. A redesign of the windows' guide-channels increased the resistance to the force of the airflow.

There is a main base and three regional bases in South Africa from which the Rolls-Royce test programmes are run. Wesinger explained: "We do our durability tests from our Johannesburg base. Usually of 30,000 kilometres' duration; two shifts, out in the morning for 600 kilometres and back at lunchtime. We download the car's computers and debrief the driver. This takes about an hour and then the car goes back out for a similar distance with the second driver. It's the same for the following days to complete a test. The cars have a satellite tracking device so that we can be sure the drivers follow the correct course, otherwise the data would less valid."

In 1910, renowned sculptor Charles Sykes created the Spirit of Ecstasy mascot for Rolls-Royce to convey the marque's unique qualities: "Speed with silence, absence of vibration, the mysterious harnessing of great energy, a beautiful, moving, living organism of superb grace." Note the temperature sensitive stickers either side of the mascot and on the bonnet top.

During the 'V Max' (maximum velocity) runs across the South African desert roads, it was found that the temperature on parts of the stainless steel bonnet reached 80 degrees Celsius (176 degrees Fahrenheit); too hot to touch. The Drophead Coupé had the same bonnet release safety catch as the Phantom, which was difficult to operate without touching the bonnet. A re-design was suggested and acted upon. The bonnet can now be opened without fear of mild burns or discomfort. Another bonnet problem was that with the sun at a low angle, too much glare was reflected into the driver's eyes. By changing the fineness of the brushing of the stainless steel, the problem was reduced to no more than a painted bonnet would cause.

Left: the testing session in South Africa revealed that light, as well as heat, was a potential source of trouble; with low sunlight reflecting glare into the driver's eyes. Modifying the finish on the stainless steel bonnet solved that problem.

Below: wherever the cars stopped on their South African test runs, they were surrounded by enthusiastic crowds. Even small boys knew the name Rolls-Royce.

The most picturesque testing region was the hill country of the Northern Cape Province. There, short runs can be made which take in a 5,000 feet climb and descent in temperatures ranging from 40 to 15 degrees Celsius (104 to 59 degrees Fahrenheit), ideal for testing engine sensors, steering and brake components and any last minute concerns a test driver might wish to address.

Wesinger's lasting memory of South Africa was that wherever they stopped for fuel or lunch, a crowd of enthusiastic and surprisingly knowledgeable local residents would appear. Many of them were boys from small villages, but they all knew the name Rolls-Royce.

The ultra-hot weather testing was undertaken in the two million acres of California's Death Valley. There, temperatures can reach 55 degrees Celsius (131 degrees Fahrenheit), with the sun beating down relentlessly with no shade in sight. From the valley floor below sea level, the test cars climbed 12,000 feet to the peaks of the High Sierras, only possible in the summer. It was the ultimate test for the computer-controlled fuel-injection system, which needed to compensate for the range of temperature and air density.

In California's Death Valley, over 1,500 kilometres were driven on dust roads to see how the hood would take the punishment. While lighter coloured cloths discoloured, the problem was solved by using a different, more durable dye.

Left: Death Valley in California is the lowest point in the New World, where temperatures can reach 55 degrees Celsius (131 degrees Fahrenheit). From there, the cars climbed 12,000 feet into the High Sierras to test the computer-controlled fuel-injection.

Opposite: the floor of Death Valley is covered in powdery borax that seeks out the slightest imperfection in a vehicle's dust-proofing. Note the incipient 'twister' making its way towards the car.

Back in Death Valley at 50 degrees Celsius (122 degrees Fahrenheit), the cars were found to be overheating. The problem was caused by the changed area and angle of the radiator compared with the Phantom saloon. A redesign of the air intakes below the radiator grille increased the air flow to match the Phantom's and all was well. While dealing with that problem, a larger radiator cooling fan replaced two smaller ones, resulting in quieter running; although more important for an open car, this system has now been adopted on the Phantom saloon.

Right and overleaf: during the exhaustive testing programme, the Drophead Coupé proved itself equal to the most demanding extremes of weather that it was likely to encounter in service, coping with everything from desert heat to a snowy Austrian winter.

In September 2006, new, stricter limits on hydrocarbon emissions were due to come into effect for California cars, and as the West Coast is seen as a major market for the Drophead Coupé, the car had to comply with these standards. The hydrocarbon emission levels are measured for the complete vehicle, not just the exhaust gases. Siegfried Wesinger explains: "The car, having run for 4,000 kilometres, is placed in an airtight room, and run on a rolling road, to mimic the way an owner might drive it. The hydrocarbons are measured from every area of the car; exhaust gas, paint, adhesives, rubber, acoustic padding, hood material, and even leather. Basically every item on the car that has an odour is tested for escaping hydrocarbons. A car must even be able to be refuelled within certain limits – the 'On Board Refuelling Vapour Recovery Test'. All these tests are extremely comprehensive and take about three weeks."

Cold weather testing was not taken to the levels that the Phantom saloon underwent as Rolls-Royce does not expect the Drophead to be used in Arctic conditions. Nevertheless, production cars may well visit ski resorts or suffer the worst of North American winters, so tests were undertaken at the temperatures ranging from -15 to 0 degrees Celsius (5 to 32 degrees Fahrenheit). The small Austrian Alpine villages of Hochgürgl and Tamsweg were chosen as bases for these tests, Wesinger reminisces: "The testing team chose these locations to avoid a lot of public attention. We didn't want to go to a place like St Moritz, where we would forever be answering people's questions and worrying about newspaper and magazine photographers. We found a friendly farmer near Hochgürgl, who would allow us to conceal the car behind his stables. From this base we could really concentrate on the job in hand."

In both handling and icing tests the Drophead Coupé performed as hoped, no major changes were required. This was an occasion when all the good work completed during the Phantom saloon's original testing period paid dividends with the design of the Drophead Coupé.

General testing, such as the effect of airflow and noise that is not specific to particular locations or conditions, was also carried out. Passengers in an open car will always suffer from airflow-buffeting due to the aerodynamic profile of the vehicle. In a car as large as the Drophead Coupé the problem is exacerbated by the distance of the rear passengers' heads from the windscreen. A conventional wind deflector was considered, but as it is not anticipated that the car will be driven at high-speed with the top down, the option was rejected, mainly due to the unattractive look of such a device. The door-mounted rear-view mirrors also proved to be a cause of unacceptable wind noise. The problem was solved by changing the profiles of the mirrors' supporting arms.

Much work was done on reducing noise levels within the car, when the hood was raised. By careful application of sound-deadening materials, the transmission of outside noise to the car's interior was dramatically reduced. Corrosion endurance tests on the many new materials used in the Drophead Coupé were condensed into a six-week period, in conditions that replicated fifteen years of normal ownership. The car was alternately driven on the road and sprayed overnight with a warm salt solution. When the car was dismantled, no unacceptable deterioration was found anywhere.

Two wheel-tyre combinations are offered on the Drophead Coupé, the Michelin PAX system and the Goodyear EMS system. The official line at Rolls-Royce is that both the Michelin and Goodyear systems are equally as good, it just depends on a customer's preference. However, if the test drivers were each given a car to keep, they would choose the French Michelin system which gives the more comfortable ride.

Above left: Rolls-Royce engineers subjected themselves to high-velocity wind-tunnel tests to ensure that passengers would enjoy a comfortable ride with the hood down. Note the adhesive tape to 're-profile' the door mirror base which initially caused airflow noise.

Above right: even Rolls-Royce motor cars have to undergo crash testing. One hopes that the dummies had a suitable sense of occasion!

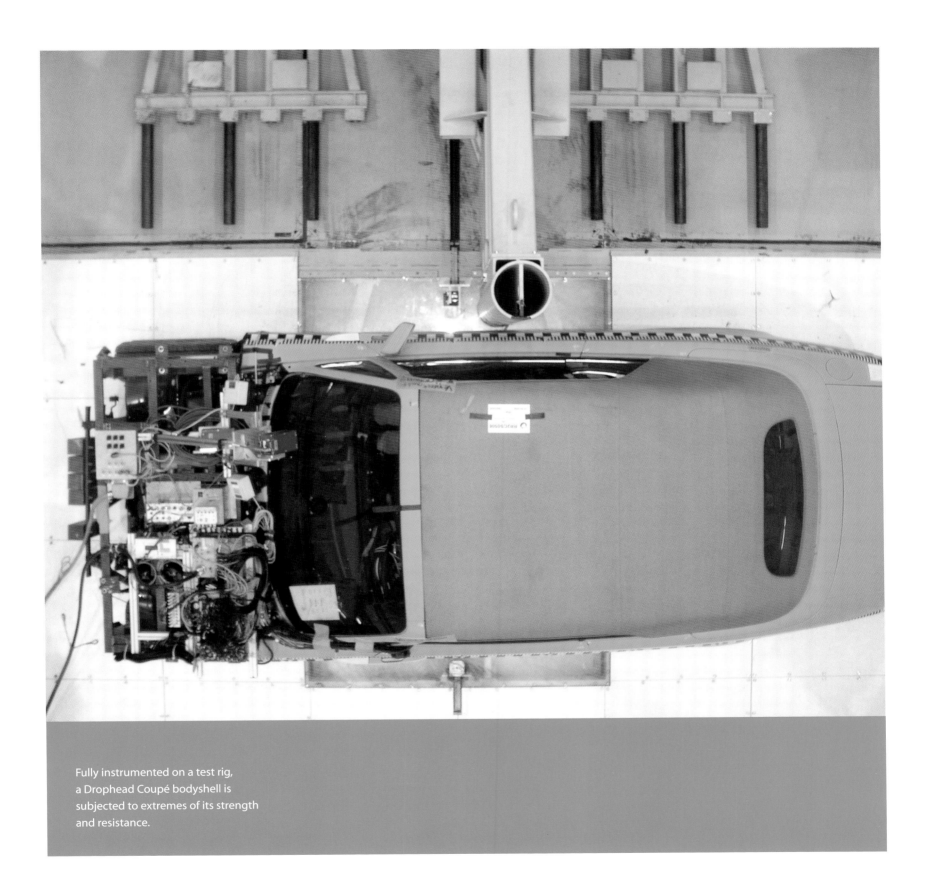

Fully instrumented on a test rig, a Drophead Coupé bodyshell is subjected to extremes of its strength and resistance.

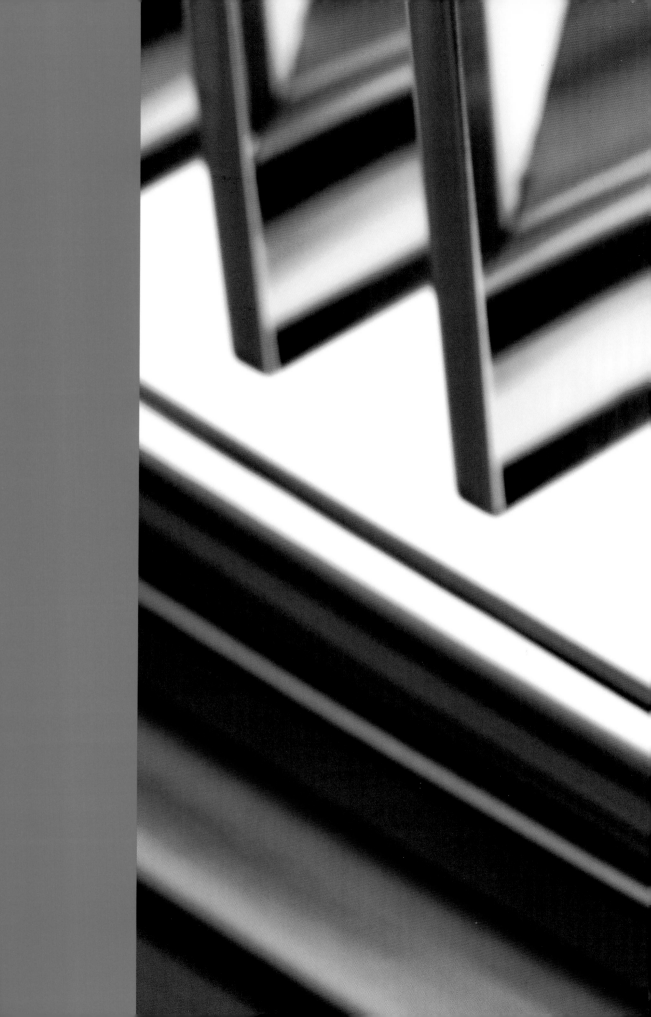

Chapter Eleven
Production Line

It's a conflict that is as old as industry: development engineers want to delay signing off a process or component for as long as possible so that they can be absolutely sure that it is as good as it can be. Production engineers want access to the procedure or component as soon as possible to make sure that it can be incorporated into the assembly process at the earliest practicable moment. It's a recurring problem.

But it's a problem in which Rolls-Royce Motor Cars has a considerable edge over large-volume car producers, explains director of engineering Helmut Riedl: "Because we are such a relatively small company, everyone knows each other well. It is much easier to overcome problems when you know how the other guy thinks and you know that you both have the same aim: to get the problem solved as quickly as possible."

Riedl was speaking of the man responsible for making sure that the Drophead Coupé could actually be built on the assembly line, former director of manufacturing Hermann Bohrer: "Hermann and I got together at a very early stage and were very open about what concerned us on the project. We always appreciated each other's point of view, which on occasions highlighted big problems; but we were always able to solve those problems. We would assemble a small team which would look at a difficulty and, rather than just saying, 'What are we going to do?' we would identify the solution first and then decide how to implement it."

The director of manufacturing has two main aspects to consider, quality and volume. Bohrer is adamant that quality must come first and volume can be gently increased as experience is gained by the workforce.

Above: still wearing its protective covers, a Drophead Coupé, fresh off the production line has the final adjustments made to the engine. From here it will move a few yards to undergo myriad tests and undergo final bodywork preparations prior to shipping.

Opposite: the point at which a mass of parts becomes a car. The jig holding the major mechanical components has been slid into place. It will now raise the engine, drivetrain, axles and wheels into place, so that the skilled operators can attach the various units.

But, he explains, sometimes the fact that a company is small can work to its disadvantage: "In a large company, if cars are coming off the production line at the rate of one a minute, an order may be placed for several thousand units of a part and after just a few days a lot of experience has been gained in fitting that part. For us, with only five or six cars a day being finished, it will be a longer learning curve."

At Goodwood, it also takes a far greater time to teach assembly workers their jobs, for instead of each person repeating a task or a small number of tasks every two or three minutes, each Rolls-Royce worker has perhaps two hours of assembly to complete. Ultimately, though, this proves far more satisfying and stimulating than the mind-numbing repetition of mass-production.

Not only was it a sound engineering decision to base the Phantom saloon on a spaceframe chassis, it was perhaps the greatest single financial aid to the whole regeneration of the Rolls-Royce Motor Cars brand. Spaceframes can easily be adapted to cater for vehicles of similar design but different dimensions, which can also share the same production line. This is not possible with the more common semi-monocoque construction of the high-volume vehicle.

It is easy to see that costs will be much lower when a single factory line is shared by two or more different models. Without this benefit, it is very likely that the business case for Rolls-Royce in general, and the Drophead Coupé in particular, could not have been made.

Above: an unusual perspective on the production line. The Drophead Coupé is the first ever production Rolls-Royce to have a sloping radiator shell.

Opposite: prior to being shipped from Dingolfing to Goodwood for surface treatment, a partially completed bodyshell reveals some of its innermost secrets.

"Every time I get out of my Rolls-Royce, everything else seems like an anti-climax"
Alfred Vanderbilt II

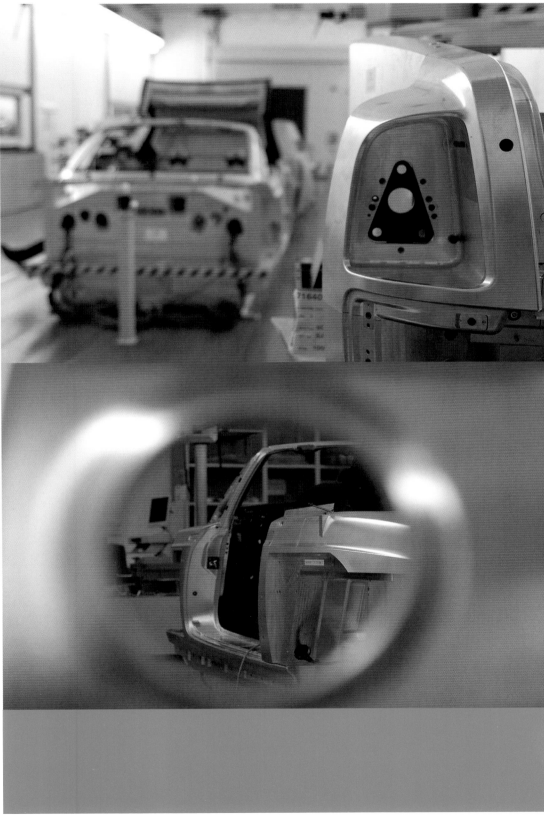

The actual build process begins with the arrival at Goodwood of the transporter trucks that bring the coated but unpainted bodyshells from the BMW Group's specialist spaceframe plant in Dingolfing, Germany. After being checked for any imperfections, the bodyshells start their journey through the 'surface treatment centre', which is much more than a traditional paint shop and uses semi-automated paint booths. Each car is painted in its chosen colour as the shell moves from booth to booth on a conveyor system.

Above: in a spray booth, a painter expertly applies the paint, under lights that show every critical angle of the body to the best effect. The air flow to the man's protective suit is pure and cool, but it is still hot work.

Right: swathed in protective coverings, this painted bodyshell has been loaded onto a cradle to begin its progress down the production line.

Above: a finished body is about to leave the surface treatment area and join the queue for the production line, where it will gain its protective covers.

Right: the production line moves forward steadily, with time allowed for the unhurried fitment of bespoke items.

When the paint process is complete, the car is pushed by hand on its trolley to a holding area where it waits to join the production line. Each bodyshell carries a number corresponding to a customer order, so that even at this early stage each car has an individual identity that can easily be tracked. It will, of course, eventually receive a vehicle identification number (VIN), but that will not be attached until the car reaches station five of the 19 stations on the line. In the case that the car is scheduled to receive special bespoke fitments that might hold up the steady flow of the production line, it can be diverted to one side to await attention. The speed of the Goodwood production line may seem snail-like by normal automotive industry standards, but there is much to do at each stage and the carefully-timed multiple tasks that must be performed by each skilled operative cannot be hurried or skimped. Quality control is all-pervading.

Enormous care is taken to avoid even the slightest scratch on any part of the car. The workforce wears clothing with concealed fastenings, while covers protect the wings and body sides. All visitors to the line must wear special protective coats and, like the workforce, must remove all jewellery and watches.

Wiring and soundproofing are the first tasks carried out on the bodyshell, along with the fitting of the chromium-plated bonnet divider. Next, pre-assembled components are added, one of the most impressively-engineered of which is the single-piece magnesium alloy instrument panel carrier.

Setting up duplicate machine shops and testbeds at Goodwood was never contemplated or considered necessary, for the simple reason that sub-assemblies such as the engine can be manufactured most efficiently at BMW Group's existing facilities.

Above: every vehicle is built to a precise order. Worksheets attached to the car's protective covering detail the special features requested by the customer, ranging from non-standard materials, finishes and colours to specialised built-in equipment.

Opposite: the powertrain is assembled on a jig that can not only be adjusted to suit the different wheelbase lengths but is so precise that in every case all the crucial bolt-holes line up when it meets the bodyshell. Here the jig is set up to fit the mechanical parts into a Phantom saloon spaceframe.

The drivetrain, which consists of everything from the radiator to the rear axle, is assembled on a separate jig-frame, which can be altered to accommodate the lengths of the saloon, the extended wheelbase car, or the Drophead Coupé. The jig-frame is then wheeled on tracks to meet the underside of the body, and the two elements are joined together.

Adjoining the pre-assembly area is the storage zone that supplies the production line with the necessary parts. Relatively few sets of components are stored, a condition of the planning consent for the site limiting the number of large lorries coming in and out of the factory. The production line is currently fed by trucks coming from the main Rolls-Royce logistics centre situated at Oxford, sixty miles away from Goodwood. The Drophead Coupé has about 1,000 different parts from the saloon, yet the Goodwood storage area has assimilated the required parts bins with very little effort or use of extra space.

Now most of the major elements such as air conditioning, electronics and the windscreen are installed on the car, the doors – which had been separated from the body after painting – are reunited with it. During this assembly process, the doors have been transported around the assembly area on upright jigs with protective sides. They have been fitted with the windows and all their electric winding mechanisms, plus the necessary locks and handles. Finally, they have received their wood and leather trim.

Opposite: because lorry deliveries to the factory are strictly limited, an adequate stock of components to meet production needs must be kept, but even so, the parts area is relatively small.

Above left: securely held in a protective jig, a trimmed door panel is fitted with the handcrafted wooden housing for its switchgear.

Above right: once the doors are trimmed and fully equipped, they will be pushed on these special trolleys to meet their bodyshell.

Opposite upper left: traditional craft skills are very much in evidence in the trim shop, one of the areas where each customer's individual wishes become reality.

Opposite upper middle: centre consoles await completion and installation.

Opposite upper right: fine woodworking is a well-established craft in West Sussex, with its long associations with ship building and furniture making.

Opposite below: the fine veneers on these panels are meticulously hand-finished.

Above left: a Rolls-Royce craftsman works diligently on a wooden panel prior to veneering and lacquering.

Above right: leather trim is hand-sewn at Goodwood, where only the very best leather available is selected for trimming Rolls-Royce motor cars.

It is doubtful that the heritage and skills of working with wood and leather to create bespoke car interiors could be surpassed outside England. Perhaps, of all the attributes appreciated in a Rolls-Royce motor car, it is the quality and use of these two natural materials that makes such a lasting impression on the senses of sight, touch and in the latter case, smell. The final assembly of the interior, therefore, is the most crucial operation; it is also the culmination of a long and varied set of skilled processes that have taken place within the leather and wood shops.

There will of course be an increase in the work necessary to add the production of the planned two or three Drophead Coupé cars per day to the existing Phantom assembly. The additional workforce will not only be needed on the production line, but on the ancillary supply areas such as surface treatment, trim and woodwork shops. It is anticipated that another two-hundred people will need to be employed to satisfy the demand for the new model.

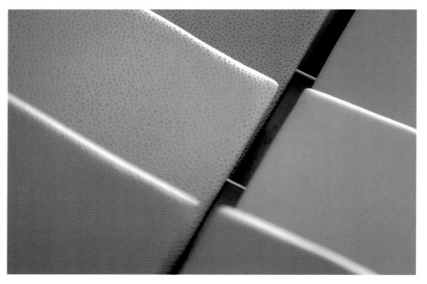

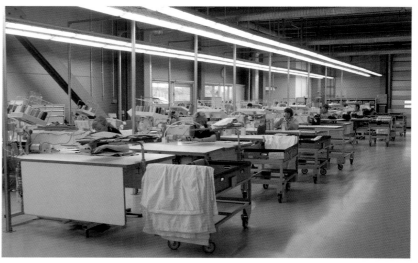

Opposite: in the leather shop, where each piece is individually cut to absolute precision having been marked-out by a computer-guided laser beam, the latest technology is married to the traditional skills that automated processes can never match.

Above: attaching leather trim to a panel with thermosensitive water-based adhesive. So effective is the fume-collection following this operation, the resultant water vapour is collected as a by-product and used to feed the pot plants in the leather-shop offices!

The hides are checked by hand and eye for any blemishes, which are marked so that they can be avoided when the leather is stretched out on a vacuum table prior to laser-guided cutting. The pattern for each of the required pieces can be repositioned by computer to maximise the use of individual hides and to work around the marked blemishes. The cut pieces, with small triangular tabs left for stitch alignment, are then skived (or shaved) along their edges if they are to be folded before stitching. Complete panels are skived if they are to cover hard surfaces without any padding.

Eduard Wenner, manager of interior trim, leather and wood, explains that these operations are a perfect example of traditional techniques being maintained while embracing the very latest technology. Certainly, to see a piece of leather being fed into a computerised, self-sharpening skiver that can reduce the material's thickness by tenths of a millimetre is extremely impressive.

However, traditional sewing machines and hand-finishing continue to be employed because these skills cannot be matched by automation. For example, absolute quality control is paramount when leather panels are stitched over airbags, yet human beings still operate the sewing machines that carry out this task, with computer monitoring merely acting as a back-up to their innate skills.

Typical of the minute care taken throughout this part of the assembly process is the fact that the thread and stitching used in making these airbag facings is weaker than that used elsewhere on the car so that, should the airbag be activated, it can burst through the stitching without the risk of it being restrained, or the hazard of flying leather lashing the faces of the occupants. Every reel of thread carries a barcode, a copy of which is embossed on the rear of the finished leather. This allows all the trim components to be traced in the event of a crash requiring analysis of the airbag deployment.

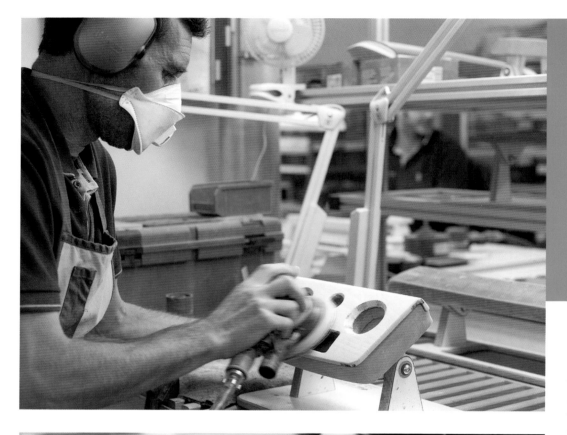

For all leather surfaces, stitched or unstitched, thermosensitive water-based glues are employed for manually attaching the leather to the base materials, whether they are padding, metal or wood. So good is the fume extraction equipment in the plant for these glues that the water collected as a by-product is used to feed pot plants around the leather shop offices; so far, all of them continue to enjoy a natural life span!

The Goodwood wood shop is as bright and spotless as the rest of the manufacturing plant. The environmentally friendly air conditioning restricts fumes from adhesive and wood dust to virtually zero. The highly-skilled craftsmen work with six different types of wood. Formed panels are composed of anything up to fifteen layers of wafer-thin wood, each one interspersed with three layers of glue film. There are also at least two layers of aluminium to aid crashworthiness and help retain the rigid form of the finished component. The glue is activated by pressing and heating the completed sections for several minutes.

Waste material is cut away and the part-finished item is sanded before suitable surface veneers are glued into place. In this case, 'suitable' means made from the customer's chosen wood, matched perfectly throughout the car. Again, waste material is trimmed and the perfectly-shaped item is sanded to form a smooth surface. Because of environmental sensitivity on the Goodwood site, the final gloss finish is applied elsewhere because the process generates some fumes.

"I recently tested a six-cylinder Rolls-Royce and it seemed, as I silently climbed hills at top speed, that my long-held dreams had suddenly come true"
Count Mortimer-Megret, 1911

An exception to this method of manufacture is the teak hood-compartment cover. Fashioned from a solid piece of teak, it is shaped, polished and oiled by hand, the required finish being a natural one, neither varnished nor lacquered. Both leather and wood 'sets' for each individual car are produced as a unique batch, and production only begins once the appropriate bodyshell is ready for painting.

The car is now ready to undergo the painstaking processes of starting, wheel-alignment and the multitude of checks and settings required by the on-board computer-monitored systems. Every completed car undergoes a 'squeak, rattle and roll' test where microphones check for the slightest noise as the car's torsional rigidity is assessed.

There is a dedicated test area for cars fitted with customer-specified non-standard electrical equipment, such as customised in-car entertainment systems.

This equipment needs careful individual integration to correct any faults and ensure that it does not conflict with any other system. A 'lab car' or test jig has been built for the company to use for this work. It also tests the suitability of any new electrical components that might enter production. Apart from looking vaguely like a real car, the 'lab car' contains all the electrical equipment found in a completely standard Rolls-Royce motor car.

When every assembly task is completed, each car is driven, then signed off to confirm that it is free of faults; those traveling abroad are then cocooned in a heat-shrink wrapped cover. A soft plastic zip gives entry to the driver's door and a small 'window' allows transport drivers to manoeuvre the car. It can now be delivered to a dealership, or moved to the customer collection room adjoining the office wing at the plant and that is where its journey into the life of a lucky new owner can truly begin.

Opposite: the unhurried production process is at an end, and a new Drophead Coupé fresh from the production line undergoes final testing and approval before being handed over to its fortunate new owner.

Above left: chief designer Ian Cameron finds a quiet corner for the final reading of his speech before the car is revealed to the expectant crowd.

Above right: sales and marketing staff prepare themselves for the inevitable questions about the Drophead Coupé.

Below right: press cameramen arrive early to get the best position for their photographs of the new Rolls-Royce.

Left: the Spirit of Ecstasy – guardian angel of the Rolls-Royce brand.

Opposite: before the new car can be launched, supporting literature has to be prepared to inform press and prospective customers. The process will have taken many weeks, with specialist staff and outside suppliers working together in an atmosphere of tight security. It is a task that, like building the cars themselves, involves many skills – writers, artists, designers, photographers, printers and bookbinders – and it all has to be ready by one immovable deadline: the world debut of the Phantom Drophead Coupé.

Another facet of the Sales and Marketing department's responsibility is the care of the Rolls-Royce Motor Cars brand. At the time the BMW Group purchased Rolls-Royce Motor Cars Ltd in 1998, the image – and therefore the brand – was tarnished. Starved of cash for many years, the old company was producing cars that were in no way as advanced or as competent as other manufactures were able to offer. Rolls-Royce Motor Cars was trading on its past days of glory and excellence far more than on its engineering prowess and quality control.

The BMW Group was fully conscious that in order to make its purchase of Rolls-Royce Motor Cars financially viable, it was imperative that their first Rolls-Royce delivered the promises that the name had always implied; myth would have to be returned to reality.

The BMW Group has an innate understanding of the importance of brand significance. Prospective customers and car enthusiasts know what a BMW is and where in the model lineup a 1, 3, 5, 6, or 7 Series car is placed; they know, too, exactly what a MINI will say about its owner. So the challenge of restoring the Rolls-Royce brand image to the very top of the motoring tree was regarded as a task in which failure was not an option. For that reason, the new Rolls-Royce Motor Cars Ltd rightly decided that they would not use or imply the century-old sobriquet 'The best car in the world', but secretly all concerned were determined to produce a car on which journalists, the public and the owners-to-be would bestow that title of their own accord. The BMW Group and Rolls-Royce knew they would only have one chance to do this, and that was to be the Phantom saloon.

Graham Biggs is director of corporate communications; he heads the department responsible for protecting and developing the reputation of Rolls-Royce Motor Cars: "We do this through many different methods. Obviously promoting the product is part of our remit, but it goes far deeper than that. We have to look at how we operate, our manufacturing processes, how we operate as a company, how successful we are, how we interact with the local community, our corporate social responsibility, even the environmental philosophy behind our factory: these are some of the many different pillars that hold up the brand image.

"Basically, our responsibility for promoting Rolls-Royce Motor Cars covers everything other than paid-for advertising, so we endeavour to educate the public through media coverage and by talking to local and national opinion formers. Our message is aimed at the general public, existing customers, potential customers, dealers, everyone working within Rolls-Royce Motor Cars and the BMW Group, local authorities, all our suppliers. But though our audience is so very wide, of course from a business point of view our primary objective is to try to stimulate sales to the best of our ability."

Giles Clayton-Jones is the company's brand manager. "We are the guardians of the Rolls-Royce Motor Cars image," he explains. "We have to look after everything that surrounds the car itself, the intangibles that complement the car: how it's sold, how we deliver facts about the car to potential and actual customers and dealers, how the car is perceived by the general public. Even the model name – a crucial point – is proposed by us."

The initial 'product positioning' document for the Drophead Coupé identified that the typical client they were aiming to attract would be a first time Rolls-Royce owner, with a stable of more than five cars, probably be male, aged over 45 and a company owner. He would have two homes, one near a coastal area. He would consider the Phantom saloon too formal and too much of a lifestyle statement. His way of life would be expressive, informal and relaxed. He would have time for emotion, beauty and the finer things in life. To attract such a buyer, it was decided that the Drophead Coupé should possess three outstanding qualities that it would communicate to its owner: elation, charisma and elegance.

Judging by the order book for the Drophead Coupé, Clayton-Jones and his colleagues underestimated the number of Phantom saloon owners who would also wish to buy a Drophead. The split between new-to-Rolls-Royce

At the Detroit Motor Show, where the Phantom Drophead Coupé was shown to the public for the first time. Left to right; Andy Thomas, Sabine Brown, Cheryl Cagle, Bob Austin, Clare Clark and Peter Miles await the onslaught of the ladies and gentlemen of the world's press.

customers and existing or previous Rolls-Royce owners is about fifty-fifty, implying that the Phantom saloon is achieving more than anyone expected for the brand and the car's owners. Clayton-Jones agrees: "Making the brand image more relevant in today's world sometimes requires us to react to peoples' perception of it as well as to create it. We can only make informed guesses as to what the customers and dealers might think. They know what they think, and if we listen, our job becomes a good deal easier."

Both Clayton-Jones and Graeme Grieve agree that although the century-old history of Rolls-Royce is a great support to the image of the brand, it should not be a mainstay of the marketing efforts. Grieve encapsulates the thinking: "We have respect for the past, but we're not anchored in it. We must bring the brand forward. After all, Royce was not relying on the past when he designed the Silver Ghost or the Phantom II Continental. Those cars were the best available in their day; why shouldn't we continue that tradition?"

With such a select customer base, mass advertising is not a cost-effective option for Rolls-Royce Motor Cars. Many of their potential customers are not susceptible to advertising, and have gatekeepers to isolate them from the many calls on their time. However, when invited by Rolls-Royce to view the experimental car '100EX' and express their opinion, they responded positively. Such people are also happy to attend lunch meetings organised by the dealerships. Typically, twenty people will attend, of whom four have already bought a car. It is not unknown for prospective customers to ask whether the owners have been paid to be so positive about their cars, a query that puts a smile on the face of Graeme Grieve!

Informed feedback is essential in the final stages of readying a new car for its launch. That is why press opinion is of paramount importance to Rolls-Royce Motor Cars, and the company takes great pride in its relationship with them. This entails trusting them to keep embargoes on press releases, which might well be announced at exciting and memorable events.

In September 2006, a select group of journalists whose opinions carry a good deal of weight within the motor industry was invited to a preview of the Drophead Coupé. After a manufacturing plant tour and lunch at Goodwood House, chairman Ian Robertson took groups of journalists for a drive in a disguised RR2 prototype. Graham Biggs suggested to his boss that he might like to take things easy, as they were in the grounds of Goodwood House. Robertson nodded his agreement, but before long he was accelerating up Goodwood's hill-climb course at over 80mph. All on board had grins on their faces, but none wider than chairman Robertson's!

Tuscany, Italy, was the chosen venue for the Press launch of the Drophead Coupé in May 2007, overseen by product public relations manager Jonathan Stanley.

Very few motorway miles were included in the selected driving routes, for the intention was to emphasise the relaxed and stress-free driving experience offered by the car and the surrounding countryside. The planning behind the event aimed to give the journalists a taste of what an owner might experience during a few days' vacation in his Drophead Coupé.

Stanley has the last word: "The car will sell itself because it looks the part and delivers an ownership experience second to none. It somehow transcends the ordinary automotive world. You can spend hours driving it, yet when you and your passengers arrive you're still totally comfortable, reminding you of just how effortless the Drophead Coupé is to live with."

Chapter Thirteen

A Tantalising Glimpse Of The Future?

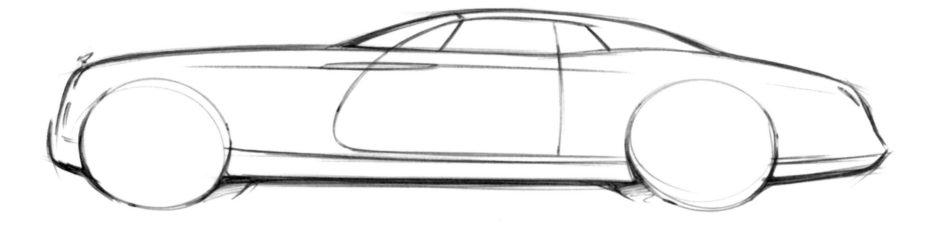

Since the first Phantom saloon was delivered to its owner, in January 2003, Rolls-Royce Motor Cars have launched an extended wheelbase version, an experimental drophead coupé named '100EX' and a production version, the Phantom Drophead Coupé; an impressive achievement for a company that has only been producing cars for a little over four years. But in February 2006, another experimental car, '101EX', was unveiled at the Geneva Motor Show. At a casual glance it is obviously similar to the open-topped car, except it is a fixed-head coupé. Apart from the addition of a solid roof structure, '101EX' has body panels made of carbon-fibre composite, attached to an aluminium spaceframe developed from that of the Phantom saloon. Various subtle styling changes have been made that differentiate it from the Drophead Coupé, all of which suit the look of this hard-topped version. If the rigidity of the drophead was impressive, then '101EX' will certainly raise eyebrows of appreciation.

An early styling sketch by Marek Djordjevic shows the desired elements of rear-hinged coach doors and large wheels, with, of course, the Rolls-Royce Spirit of Ecstasy mascot.

Above right: the interior lighting arrangement in '101EX' is something special. As well as the variable mood lighting that it shares with the Drophead Coupé, the ambience is further enhanced by pin-points of fibre optic lights housed in the leather rooflining. Here they are set at a brightness that would not disturb a driver, but would reflect a soft glow onto the faces of the chatting passengers.

Below right: the 'starlight headliner' shows the rear compartment in brilliance that passengers could happily read by. Of course if they were about to arrive at a show business awards event, then the starlight headliner would not harm their chances of being seen at all.

Alan Sheppard and Charles Coldham were responsible for the interior design, which is a plush place indeed for one to sit. With the expected rear-quarter mirrors, mounted in the 'C pillars', between the side windows and the rear screen and 'lounge' seating, rear passengers experience a real sense of privacy. This is in no way claustrophobic, as the side-windows wind down completely, without a supporting pillar between the front and rear glass. Front passengers who have experience of the drophead will feel right at home, except for the substitution of more traditional upholstery materials that need not cater for the potential water ingress and humidity of an open car.

Drophead Coupé-like interior lighting is supplemented by a myriad of tiny fibre optics embedded in the leather headlining. Operated by a dimmer-switch they can illuminate from the setting of 'a star-filled night sky' through a soft glow, to an intensity that is bright enough to read by. Charles Coldham explains his objective. "Innovative cabin lighting provides a hospitable glow, the perfect backdrop for a conversation." With the use of a solid roof, the rear and side windows are framed in rosewood and red oak veneers, a feature used by the great coachbuilders of the past.

If there is a weakness with the design, then it is the meeting of the polished stainless steel windscreen surround and the painted hard-top, as from some angles the striking visual differences in the two surfaces seem at odds with one another. Much as the Drophead coupé design has the teak used on the hood-cover extended along the door tops, perhaps bright metal or paint could merge more gently at screen frame and roofline.

Above: a moody studio photograph shows off the balance of curves and razor edge profiles that designers Cameron and Djordjevic have conjured from their imaginations. If '101EX' were music, then it would be a symphony.

Opposite: below the waistline, '101EX' shares the look of the Drophead Coupé, save for the exhaust pipe trims, hewn from solid alloy. The hunched stance of the car gives a distinct promise of unleashed power, even when waiting at the kerbside.

Above: when just the front of '101EX' is in view, it could be mistaken for a Drophead Coupé, as the contours of the bodywork, the assimilation of the classic Rolls-Royce radiator and the lighting arrangement are exactly the same.

Right: a fast moving car and a slow camera shutter setting give an impression of speed as '101EX' crosses the Anderson bridge in Singapore. Rest assured, at whatever speed '101EX' travels, those linked 'R-R' motifs on the wheel centres will remain upright.

Just as they did with '100EX', Rolls-Royce Motor Cars have stated that there are currently no plans to put '101EX' into production, which in the writers view is a great shame. Having achieved so much with the testing, design and execution of the existing production cars, it would seem wise to realize the potential for the small but rewarding market sector that needs such a car as '101EX'. If, as in Ian Cameron's words "it matches the elegance and romance of yesterday with the technology of tomorrow," then such a car would surely be in demand.

Postscript

'This book has been produced independently of Rolls-Royce Motor Cars Ltd, and so I have been under no obligation to enhance the good or glaze over the not so good facts about the Phantom. I was able to approach the project with a completely neutral view, although it was my fervent wish that I would find the marque of Rolls-Royce to be in safe hands. With no guarantee or control over the contents of this book, both Rolls-Royce Motor Cars and the BMW Group have allowed me complete access to facilities, personnel and records concerning Project Rolls-Royce, the making of the Phantom saloon, for which I thank them unreservedly.'

So wrote I in the postscript to the Goodwood Phantom. The same holds true for this book, concerning the Phantom Drophead Coupé. My problem remains the same, and that is the worry of appearing sycophantic about the new Rolls-Royce Motor Cars Ltd and their products, but there is no alternative other than to avoid the truth about what the company has achieved in its short life. The company structure, especially its close but autonomous relationship with the BMW Group; the exemplary manufacturing plant and head office complex at Goodwood; the attraction of a highly talented design, engineering and assembly workforce; and the cars themselves, including the two experimental models, are witness enough to what has been accomplished.

The new company has, since 2003 been able to re-instate the image of Rolls-Royce cars to the top of the automotive tree. Public perception has changed from grudging acceptance of an historic but tarnished name, to open admiration for the best of automotive engineering. The cars are a product of worldwide talent, but are seen as being quintessentially British, with the epitome of engineering excellence proudly shown; the Spirit of Ecstasy mascot, the Rolls-Royce radiator grille and the linked 'R-R' letters, front and rear.

Is the Phantom Drophead Coupé an outstanding car? Yes it is, if you want supreme comfort, luxury taken to a new level by the shear quality of construction, and a driving and passenger experience second to none - if formula one racing-performance is not your desire.

The order book for the Coupé is bursting its covers. The first car has been sold, although delivery will not be until late summer. The buyer bid for it at the Naples Winter Wine Festival charity auction, in Florida, USA. It fetched the highest price ever paid for a new car in America; two million dollars, of which most will go to children's charities. It would seem that Rolls-Royce Motor Cars have another winning model.

DESIGN	Ben Gibbs, Motion Design
PRINTER	Star Standard Industries Pte Ltd., Singapore
PRINTING	Four color litho on Roland Speedmaster
PAGE SIZE	280mm x 280mm
TEXT PAPER	170 gsm Stora Enso Matt Art
END PAPERS	140 gsm Woodfree
DUST JACKET	150 gsm Glossy Art
INKS	Toyochem
CASING	Wibalin
BODY TEXT	9/13pt Sabon & Myriad